America's Great
Social and Healthcare
Reformer

Paul M. Kaplan

PELICAN PUBLISHING COMPANY
GRETNA 2018

For Kyle and Julian Rozanes

The word "Pelican" and the depiction of a pelican are
trademarks of Pelican Publishing Company, Inc., and are
registered in the U.S. Patent and Trademark Office.

Library of Congress Cataloging-in-Publication Data

Names: Kaplan, Paul M., author.
Title: Lillian Wald : America's great social and healthcare reformer / Paul
  M. Kaplan.
Description: Gretna : Pelican Publishing Company, [2018] | Includes
  bibliographical references and index.
Identifiers: LCCN 2017033545| ISBN 9781455623495 (hardcover : alk. paper) |
  ISBN 9781455623501 (ebook)
Subjects: LCSH: Wald, Lillian D., 1867-1940--Juvenile literature. | Social
  reformers--New York (State)--New York--Juvenile literature. | Public
  health nurses--New York (State)--New York--Juvenile literature. | Henry
  Street Settlement (New York, N.Y.)
Classification: LCC HQ1413.W34 K37 2018 | DDC 362.5092 [B] --dc23 LC
record available at https://lccn.loc.gov/2017033545

Printed in the United States of America

Published by Pelican Publishing Company, Inc.
1000 Burmaster Street, Gretna, Louisiana 70053
www.pelicanpub.com

Contents

Preface

They say one person can't change the world. Yet, there are those who have tried and largely succeeded. Often, it take a different perspective, the courage to try something different and the skills to put that vison into action. It also takes stellar influencing skills to convince funders and partners to join.

Lillian Wald is noted as one of the least known, yet most important people of her time. President Franklin D. Roosevelt noted that in his 1937 radio address about her.

Starting as a young nurse in New York City, Lillian felt the field was too mechanical. It did not address patients in a dignified way. Nor did it address their underlying needs. Still yet, the task was not just curing them but about ameliorating the societal issues that often contributed to disease and suffering. From this, the field of nursing, social work, and public health spawned.

Teaching a class in the Lower East Side, the most densely packed neighborhood in the world at the time, she made a realization that would change her and those around her forever. She decided she would live in the neighborhood she was serving. Rarely done before, she left the security of a nursing job and along with her classmate moved into the neighborhood and opened up her impromptu practice. She convinced a philanthropic family to fund her efforts. It became among the first "settlements."

Soon after, it became apparent that health needs were just one part of the puzzle. The population she sought to help were bogged down by very low-paying and long-hour jobs with little or no protection for workers. The need for worker's rights and labor strikes for reform rose to the surface. But this caused conflict among the Henry Street Settlement's donors. Many of them felt that giving money for healthcare needs was fine—but not to labor reforms. Lillian Wald and her Settlement were in a moral bind: fight for labor reforms or keep the donations flowing.

This bind was most apparent during the US entry to into World War I. Lillian and many nurses at the Settlement opposed the US entering the War. This put her at odds with her backers—not to mention her personal relationship with the US president at the time, Woodrow Wilson. The conflict highlights larger questions about charities. When does an organization become political? What if it contrasts with those supporting it? What is a charity's role in resolving political and economic conflicts?

Lillian and her Henry Street Settlement challenged the status quo, racial integration, and gender equality as well. Somewhat unusual at the time, Settlement classes integrated black and white students. The organization that would become the National Association for the Advancement of Colored People (NAACP) was born in the Henry Street Settlement's dining room. On the gender equality front, she and her staff marched for obtaining the right to vote for women and supported efforts eventually leading to the passage of the Nineteenth Amendment.

Another aspect ahead of its time was the notion of treating the "whole" person. Looking beyond patients' symptoms, Lillian recognized the need for people to express themselves artistically. From this idea spawned the Grand Street Playhouse where neighborhood residents and professional artists alike have performed. That theater today is over a century old.

What's remarkable about this story is that many of these themes from over a century ago are today's headlines. Society still grapples with issues around immigration, gender and racial equality, labor reform, worker rights, and much more. Still, Lillian and her team are to thank for school nurses, school lunches, playgrounds, advancement of nursing and public health, artistry as part of enrichment programs, and social services advancements.

Indeed, this narrative is not simply about one woman nor even just about the Henry Street Settlement or Visiting Nurse Service. Rather, it is a story about America—how the country has struggled to evolve in the face of multiple conflicts. From that, we can draw contemporary lessons.

Enjoy the story.

Acknowledgments

I am grateful for the input and support from many people and institutions who made this project possible.

I thank Susan LaRosa, Deputy Officer, Marketing and Communications at Henry Street Settlement for her guidance, support, and sharing of photos. I also thank the archives at the New York Public Library, the Museum of the City of New York, and the Health Sciences Library at Columbia University for helping me research their archives and select and scan photos.

I also thank authors of previous biographies of Lillian Wald and Jacob Riis.

I also salute Amy Stein-Milford and Hanna Griff of the Museum at Eldridge Street as well as Laurie Tobias Cohen and Lori Weissman at the Lower East Side Jewish Conservancy and the Jewish Book Council for their partnership in promoting cultural history and experiences to the public. I also thank Christina Kasman at the Yale Club library for her support. I spent many days writing in the tranquil library.

A project as intensive as this is better served with the support of family and friends. I wish to also thank Barney Pearson for his close friendship and work on this book, Laura-Jeanne Monahos for her solid emotional support and ideas, and Jacob Koskimaki for his ongoing encouragement and dialogue around writing.

I am thankful to my parents Jack and Eileen, my brother Andrew Kaplan, my uncle Ted Katz, the entire Rozanes family, and my cousins Diane and Ed Ziegman and Robert and Jane Katz. I also acknowledge the encouragement of other friends: Miguel Barrios, Howard Brayer, Jiyoung Cha, Paul Donnelly, Sharon Goldman, Alfred Robert Hogan, Olga Hopkins, Ron Klayman, Bonnie Kintzer, Sumesh Madan, Ben Manalaysay, Angela Pruitt, Karen Seiger, and Felix Kaplan. I'm also thankful to the staff at Gotham Writing.

Finally, a shout out to the team at Pelican Publishing: Kathleen

Calhoun Nettleton, President and Publisher for supporting this project; the talented editor-in-chief Nina Kooij and editor Eugenie Brignac; promotion director Antoinette de Alteriis; sales director Don Anderson; and Ty Varnado, education sales manager.

Chapter 1

The Early Years

Of all the efforts in helping the poor, few succeeded more than the one that sprang from a single young woman named Lillian Wald.

Her name is little known, but she changed the nation in a way few could. She transformed healthcare and brought medical attention to those who needed it most. She helped stop abuses of workers and children in the workplace. She championed the rights of children. School nurses, free school lunches, special education, community nursing, and healthcare were all causes she advanced. She transformed the way society treats the sick and the poor. Changes that last to this day.

Yet, Lillian Wald came from an unlikely background to become one of the country's greatest reformers. She grew up in the 1870s-'80s in an environment far away from the tumult of the Lower East Side she would one day serve. In fact, Lillian had little contact with the poor during her childhood. The poor were another world—people unknown to her who lived in slums and toiled in factories.

But the future reformer grew up knowing little of that. Her grandparents were immigrants to the US from Germany. Both her parents' ancestors lived harmoniously in their homeland. Yet, they sought more opportunity in the rapidly growing US. Like so many at the time, they brought with them a culture and the strength and idealism which they hoped to make the most of in the US. Lillian's Jewish ancestors settled in the US easily. They would become prosperous businesspeople and highly regarded members of their new communities.

Her father, Max Wald, was a quiet man focused on providing for his family. Lillian was somewhat distant from him, as he did not smile easily. He was a dealer in the optical business. At the time, Rochester, New York was known for optics and imaging. It is the city where Eastman Kodak and Baush & Lomb were founded.

Her uncle also lived with the family. Uncle Sam had a brilliant career in medicine. Yet, it was short-lived. One day, he swallowed more of a self-prescribed medicine than he had intended. He was hurt physically by the overdose. But the scars were emotional too. He lost his confidence in prescribing medicine to others.

He came to stay with the Walds often. Despite his wounds, he was jovial with Lillian and her three siblings. He introduced them to the theater, music, and literature and was said to spoil them with elaborate toys and ponies.

Lillian always had a special relationship with her brother Alfred. He made her his partner and confidant. He had considered becoming a doctor. But his plans shifted when he entered the family business.

Outside her sheltered life in Rochester, New York in the 1870s, major social movements in labor and women's equality were afoot. Emma Goldman, an immigrant from Russia, complained of intolerable and oppressive work conditions. Living in Rochester, Emma worked for ten and a half hours per day for six weeks and could not even cover her room and board. These conditions enraged her. She began to talk of unions with other workers in secret. They demanded an eight hour workday. As Lillian was in her teens, worker strikes broke out to all factories including those owned by Lillian's uncles.

While these labor strikes were growing, Susan B. Anthony and Elizabeth Cady Stanton were fighting for women's rights. Not far from Lillian's home in Rochester, history had been made just decades prior. In Seneca Falls, New York, women suffrage activists declared at the Seneca Falls Convention of 1848 the importance of giving women nationwide the right to vote. When Wald was a teenager, Anthony and Stanton formed the National Woman Suffrage Association. They also fought for property rights for married women. Their vision for a federal amendment granting all women the right to vote would not occur until 1920. But in the intervening years, there were many protests and demonstrations. Demands for a more just social order were growing louder.

Lillian was exposed to some of this thought when her grandfather took her to hear the famed minister Henry Ward Beecher, an outspoken supporter of women's suffrage. When Wald was around twelve years old, the National Suffrage Association held its annual meeting in Rochester with Frederick Douglass, Susan B. Anthony, Lucretia Mott, and Elizabeth Cady Stanton present. Other campaigns focused on opening up the nearby University of Rochester to women.

In 1851, Susan B. Anthony and Elizabeth Cady Stanton entered into a famed partnership that transformed the political and social condition of American women—and by extension, women around the globe. They spearheaded the first women's rights convention in Seneca Falls in upstate New York in July 1848. Here, Stanton expounded her Declaration of Rights and Sentiments invoking equal rights such as the right to vote. Stanton and Anthony were both anti-slavery and therefore encountered hostile audiences at their speeches.

She sought changes in her own life too. She was studying at Miss Martha Cruttenden's English and French Boarding and Day School for Young Ladies and Little Girls. Their moto was to "make scholarly women and womanly scholars." Growing bored with her studies at Miss Cruttenden's school, she decided she would apply to college early.

One day at the age of sixteen, in a burst of assertiveness, Lillian announced she was going to apply to college. That was an unusual move for a woman at this time. Her mother had always planned for her to get married and raise a family nearby.

Lillian announced that she was applying to Vassar, unusual given her young age. In fact, Vassar did admit students at fifteen years of age if they fulfilled the entrance requirements. But not always. Weeks later, Lillian would learn that Vassar College decided she was too young to attend. The president of the college suggested that she continue her studies and that when she was older, he may reconsider her application. Then, tragedy struck.

Lillian received a telegram that her brother Alfred had drowned. His life had ended quickly. She felt like hers had too. Sadness beset the Wald family for years. Lillian later wrote that her mother's eyes "took on a sadness that they never lost again."[1]

Portrait of early women's suffrage leader Susan B. Anthony in Rochester, N.Y. around 1855. History of Woman Suffrage *by Anthony and Elizabeth Cady Stanton,* Volume I, *published in 1881.*

Organized protest for women to receive the right to vote, circa 1917. (Courtesy of the Visiting Nurse Service of New York Records, Archives & Special Collections, Health Sciences Library, Columbia University.)

Lillian's dreams were shattered. Her relationship with Alfred was more than that of siblings. She had imagined they would work and study together. Her future was intertwined with his.

Lillian changed course. She realized how much her mother was hurting. With her sister, Julia, married and out of the house, she wanted to become the faithful daughter. She attended parties that had the unspoken purpose of her meeting her future husband. Her mother wanted to see her settled in the life she imagined for her.

She met several suitors. She liked them. Yet, she did not want to commit herself to marriage. She could not shake the feeling that she was meant to do something else. But what? Was it finding employment? She briefly worked as a correspondent for the Bradstreet Company (today, Dun & Bradstreet). Her responsibility was to write down anything she could find on a company's credit rating and financial status. This information was then sold to brokers or investors.

The work was fairly easy. She was happy to be exercising her curiosity in this new field. Yet, she eventually grew bored with writing the reports.

Then a course of events would show Lillian the path she was meant to take. She was visiting her sister Julia at the seashore when Julia became ill. They called for a doctor, who summoned for a nurse. Lillian was asked to fetch the nurse. Lillian walked the nurse back to the house, and asked her many questions. Lillian hadn't met any woman with her background. The nurse had trained at Bellevue Hospital in New York, the first hospital in the US to offer nurse training. She seemed to know much about therapeutic practices.

For the first time, Lillian could see herself in this young nurse. She knew what she wanted to do. She was to become a nurse. Her family had mixed emotions. But if they were to support this decision, they wanted her to at least stay in Rochester.

Yet, Lillian marched to her own beat. In early 1889, she applied to nursing school in New York at the age of twenty-two. Yet, the minimum age requirement was twenty-five. She decided that the ends justified the means and lied about her birth year. She used her sister's birth year of three years earlier.

Her interest stemmed less from an empathy for the sick and more about her need to feel useful and to find a fulfilling career. She longed for that. She never felt at home among her peers in Rochester. She defied conventions. But she herself was not sure what she wanted instead. Nursing gave her that window.

Chapter 2

The Nurse to-Be

Lillian's vision started to be realized. She came to New York City for an interview at the School of Nursing at New York Hospital. As she exited the cab and arrived at the door of the formidable building on a summer's day in 1889, she had concerns about whether she would interview well. She turned to her brother-in-law, Charles Barry, for sympathy.

Barry wanted to support his sister-in-law. But another part of him wanted Lillian to give up this nursing idea and return home to Rochester, New York. She could settle down like most girls, he thought, and her family would be relieved.

Once inside, she met with Miss Sutliffe, the administrator. Interviewing Lillian, she glanced at her essay. "My life till now has been a type of modern American young womanhood, days devoted to society, study and housekeeping duties such as practical mothers consider essential to a daughter's education. This does not satisfy me now. I feel the need of serious, definite work, a need perhaps more apparent since the desire to become a professional nurse has had birth."[1]

Miss Sutliffe had a positive feeling about Wald. But she was also concerned that she may be too "impassioned" for the job. She offered to take Lillian on a tour of the hospital.

The hallways were drab. The white walls were plain plaster. Sounds of groans and sighs echoed. The smell of cleaning powders pervaded.

When visiting the children's section, she noticed a young boy in braces. She felt pity for him. But the nurse administrator caught Lillian's reaction and gave her the first important test in nursing. "That boy is not suffering. He's proud of being here and of having the most elegant 'bandages' of anyone," she said. "He is a hero in the ward, and if you come you and he will have great fun together."[2] Lillian realized the difference between pity and acceptance of a difficult situation.

Lillian was eager to be accepted and embark on her life's work as a nurse. Quite eager. When her interview was over, Lillian exited the hospital with her brother-in-law. Miss Sutliffe watched her with curiosity. She wondered if Lillian would change her mind and lead a more conventional life. Yet, she noticed something determined about the way Lillian walked. A quiet passion. She knew she would see Lillian again.

But she could not have known that one of the greatest healthcare, education, and labor reformers had just walked out her door.

Lillian was accepted by the New York School of Nursing in August 1889, and she returned to New York to embark on her new path. Her life in the hospital was a dose of reality. Many of her tasks were menial, and she often worked twelve hour days. She wished she could interact more with patients.

After a few days, she made a grave mistake. Lillian went to the basement on an errand and heard wild shouting from a locked room. Worried, she rushed to the door and found an elderly man in a padded cell yelling that he was starving. He said he had not been fed in days. Furious, she convinced the elevator man to let her into the kitchen where she took prepared food to the starving man. She felt proud. She had helped a needy patient. Or so she thought.

The next day she burst into Miss Sutliffe's office. She spoke rapidly and almost incomprehensibly. She told of this injustice to a displeased Miss Sutliffe.

Irritated, yet at the same time admiring Lillian's determination, Miss Sutliffe set the record straight. She explained that patients in that corridor were brought to the hospital because they were drinking heavily. They became ill and unmanageable. So, the hospital needed to set apart these unruly patients until they sobered up. Otherwise, they could annoy or even harm other patients.

Miss Sutliffe paused and glanced at the floor. She looked disappointed about what she was to say next. She noted that the kitchen staff was "wondering about the strange disappearance of several items from the icebox."[3]

But Miss Sutliffe also offered her words of encouragement. She said she was glad Lillian cared for the patients, even if it was misguided.

Lillian felt misunderstood. She wanted to help patients in need and not let regulations get in the way. That would serve her later in her famed life. But, for now, she realized she needed to understand and advocate for gradual changes in regulations.

Lillian Wald exited the office and stepped into her newfound confidence as a nurse.

Over the next year and a half, Miss Wald grew into her newfound profession. The "sisterhood," as nursing was called, suited her. She made lifelong friends. She felt like she fit in. She wanted to understand the "long words" doctors would use. Or to answer questions like why the corners of the building were round.

Nurses back then received little training by today's standards. Most learning was done by doing rather than through lectures and textbook reading. In fact, decades prior to Lillian's enrollment, the idea of teaching women to care for the sick was laughed at. It was the ground-breaking English nurse, Florence Nightingale, who surprised all by declaring that women need to be formally taught in this profession. It was the urgency of war and its injured soldiers that advanced Florence's belief about nursing education.

Lillian loved interacting with patients where she could. But the hospital management seemed to frown on it. It seemed to her to be consumed with rigid

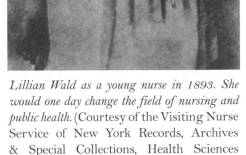

Lillian Wald as a young nurse in 1893. She would one day change the field of nursing and public health. (Courtesy of the Visiting Nurse Service of New York Records, Archives & Special Collections, Health Sciences Library, Columbia University.)

restrictions. Everything had to be done precisely—when patients' temperatures were taken, when food was to be eaten, etc.

One day, Lillian relayed to a doctor a light moment she shared with a patient. "I told Mr. Anderson, the patient, a funny story, and he laughed. Really laughed. I think you'll find him much more cheerful."

The doctor was unamused. He stared at her with an annoyed expression. "Laughter is likely to be a strain on him just now. When humor is indicated, I shall prescribe it. Nurse, what is his temperature?"[4]

Florence Nightingale, a social reformer from England, is considered the founder of professional nursing. During the Crimean War in Europe (1853-1856), she was known as "the Lady with the Lamp" as she visited wounded soldiers in the dark of night. She later advanced the field through founding one of the first nursing schools around the globe. She was also known as a statistician and writer of mystical religious topics.

Lillian had forgotten to take the patient's temperature, but she had remembered to make him laugh. To make him feel human. That would win her no favors at the hospital. But what she could not have known is that her empathy would one day make her change nursing forever. But, at this point, she had to deal with dozens of regulations. She disliked following them but for now she had little choice.

Patients appreciated Lillian. They would say to each other that she treated them like an individual. They did not feel like another anonymous patient with a list of tasks to complete.

One patient expressed this sentiment. "She doesn't make you feel you've committed a crime by getting sick and needin' more help than you can pay for."

Eventually, her graduation came. Miss Sutliffe smiled upon seeing her graduate. She knew she was right about Lillian from that first interview. She suspected that Lillian, though, would not live within the confines of nursing at a hospital for the remainder of her career.

But life back in Rochester was calling. In May 1891, she received tragic news. Her father had died. Lillian was pained just like she had been when her brother Albert died several years earlier. On her journey home, she felt torn. She felt free in New York and rising in her profession. Yet, she was tormented to think of her mother's anguish as a new widow. She considered moving back home. Many emotional family discussions about the future for their mother ensued. Eventually, it was settled. Mrs. Wald would move in with her other daughter, Julia, and son-in-law. After a few months of helping her mother, Lillian returned to New York to undertake her first job as a professional nurse.

Back in New York and done with training, she was able to choose her first job as a nurse. She wanted to work with children. She embarked on her new position as a staff nurse at the New York Juvenile Asylum.

This institution had been established about four decades earlier to "care for and take charge of all truant, disobedient, friendless, and neglected children of both sexes between ages seven and fourteen." Located in what was then a rural area in northern Manhattan, the asylum had a prison-like feel. The walls were high, and it seemed cut-off from everything. It was not a happy place. The children were not allowed outdoors much, except to perform particular duties.

The children at the asylum were generally unruly. Many had committed crimes and had no qualms about passing on their secrets of lawbreaking to each other. Lillian had a different take on these youngsters than other staff members. Whereas most wrote them off as troublemakers and "bad kids," Lillian believed that it was not their fault they stole in order to eat or to have "a little excitement in their lives." She believed society's ills were at the root of the problem. Moreover, orphaned children were "thrown together" with petty criminals at the asylum to discipline them. She also felt the asylum staff was at fault for their indifference towards the children.

Just as in her training, Lillian clashed with the institution's rigid regulations. One day, a boy had a painful toothache so Lillian rushed him to the institution's dentist. Whereas her instructions were simply to "take him to the dentist," she stayed with him. The dentist quickly noted that he would need to extract the tooth. "How would he know so quickly?" she thought. He did not even examine the boy's mouth. She felt herself get angry at this injustice. She could not keep silent.

She scolded the dentist for so hastily deciding to pull the boy's tooth without trying to save it. He could have lost his tooth unnecessarily. She threatened to take the boy to her own dentist. Then, the dentist relented. He agreed to examine the boy. He determined that he was able to save the tooth.

Lillian felt vindicated. But after months of similar incidents she felt overwhelmed. She could not swim upstream any longer. The institution was overwhelming. She realized a certain truth: "Even if the asylum itself were vastly improved, it would never be a satisfactory place for children to grow up in."[5] Society needed to be reformed. These places were only addressing the symptoms. And they were barely doing that.

After a year, she decided to leave the asylum and return to school. She enrolled in the Woman's Medical College for the fall term of 1892. She had just turned twenty-five. Her studies consisted of physics, chemistry, anatomy, physiology, and lab work. She studied intensely, but missed the company of her friends.

Each day when she left her student dorm, she witnessed lines of poor sick people patiently waiting to enter the infirmary. The world of the poor started to feel more real. Not like back in Rochester when she was sheltered from it. What was once an abstraction was now reality. She wrote that she observed "visibly distressed men, women, and children in ragged clothes, women with sick babies in their arms and their flushed, feverish faces, running noses and heard their coughs."[6]

She wanted more interaction with patients. She felt her studies were too confining. Sometimes, on a park bench she would speak to those visiting the hospital. Lillian would perform an "on the spot" exam—not sanctioned by the hospital—and make suggestions on care. She also realized that most did not trust hospitals. They were places of pain, where loved ones had died, where the staff seemed cold and uncaring.

Venturing out from her medical classroom, Miss Wald volunteered to teach a class in home care and hygiene for Jewish immigrant women. Mrs. Betty Loeb, the wife of a wealthy financier, was a noted philanthropist. She funded this effort to teach the class. Lillian traveled to the Lower East Side of New York to teach at the Louis Technical School at 267 Henry Street. Lillian had never traveled to this neighborhood before. She saw great poverty that she had never witnessed. Immigrants were packed into dark, airless tenement rooms often with broken-down wooden stairs and no indoor plumbing. The streets were packed with shops, pushcarts and peddlers hawking their items. She witnessed children playing in garbage. It was the most densely packed neighborhood in the world. The noise and smell assaulted her senses. She had never known this kind of life existed back in her middle-class neighborhood in Rochester. This was a world away.

She realized her own ignorance. Yes, she had worked with needy patients before. But nothing like this. Most students spoke limited English and gave blank stares when Lillian spoke. After several lessons, Lillian "got the hint" and began speaking in simpler English. She taught them lessons on hygiene and good health. She felt empathy towards her students. She wanted to see each one as an individual. Her previous employers would often see all them in one way: "those poor" or "the disadvantaged." But she also remembered a lesson she had first learned in nursing school. What is needed is not pity, but rather a practical solution.

Then one day while she was teaching Lillian's life changed.

Chapter 3

A New Kind of Nurse

While teaching her class, a weeping child sheepishly entered the room. Lillian looked up from her bed making demonstration. A tense silence fell on the room.

"Your mother is sick. Is that it?" Lillian asked.[1]

The child nodded.

Sensing the urgency, Lillian dismissed the class and followed the child into the chaotic neighborhood over broken-down roads and foul smelling uncovered garbage cans. Lillian had to hold the bundle of sheets against her nose as she went by. She had no idea what she was going to encounter.

She finally reached a dilapidated tenement where she climbed up muddy steps in a dark hallway. The floors creaked. Odors defiled the hallways. Lillian could barely see anything ahead of her due to the poor lighting. She held tightly to the broken railing in order to keep her balance. The child stopped and opened a door. She finally entered a two-room apartment where she found a young woman lying in bed in a dingy room. There was no heat and virtually no light.

The child pointed to her mother. Lillian saw in the distance a sick woman lying down. She hemorrhaged when she had given birth two days prior. Dried blood covered her. A family of seven crowded in the two rooms in addition to those whom they leased tiny amounts of space to in order to pay rent.

Lillian was horrified. She had never seen anything like it. She would later call this incident "baptism by fire." She cared for the sick woman and the new baby. She reassured the anguished family. She not only cared for their medical needs but also for their hygiene needs. She placed fresh sheets on the soiled bed and scrubbed the hard-worn floors. She cooked them a simple meal. As she was leaving the tenement, she paused. She turned towards the frightened family and promised to return. They kissed her hand in gratitude.

This would mark a fundamental change for Lillian. She rethought her life's work. No longer did she see herself as "just a nurse" or a part of an institution. Nor was she content with simply teaching hygiene classes to immigrants. She wanted to care for the sick but also change the social conditions that led to the abject poverty and unseemly conditions. Amidst the poverty surrounding her, she found a way to utilize her studies. She also had another realization. The public did not know about these horrid conditions. If they did, she reasoned, more would be done to ameliorate suffering.

She had found where she was needed.

That night, she barely slept. She reflected on all she saw that day. She had never seen such a scene. No one back in Rochester told her how the poor lived. It was never taught in her studies at Miss Cruttenden's School. She felt compelled to help the needy. But how? And who would pay for it?

Disenchanted with her studies, which she now saw as irrelevant, she dropped out of medical college. She decided to try something radical. She decided to move in to the neighborhood that she was to serve. She was to move to the Lower East Side, the most densely packed area in the world at the time. No longer was she serving the poor and disenfranchised from afar. It would be part of her daily routine. But she needed a partner. She found a kindred spirit in her classmate Mary Brewster. The two young medical practitioners devised a plan that had little precedent in nursing. They would live among the poor, locate sick people, and nurse them in their own homes.

How would they fund this venture? Lillian proved to have not only great nursing abilities but also financial acumen. She turned again to Mrs. Betty Loeb, the philanthropist funding her hygiene class. This time, her ask was far greater. Mrs. Loeb was more accustomed to funding the arts but grew excited about this venture. Miss Wald visited her at home to make the request.

Lillian told Mrs. Loeb of what she had seen, as though no one in the world knew about this poverty. She lamented that these immigrants had come for a better life yet have only found "filth and degradation."

Mrs. Loeb was taken aback. Not by the young nurse's enthusiasm. She expected that. But the way in which she presented her case. As a philanthropist, Mrs. Loeb was accustomed to solicitors asking for donations to "charity." By charity, they meant giving the poor money for basic needs but not helping them improve their situations. Certainly, none of them demanded a change to the economic system of fairness.

The philanthropist looked Miss Wald over and saw that determined expression on her face. She was intrigued by her passion.

Mrs. Loeb asked Lillian if she wanted money for the family. But Lillian explained that she had something much bigger in mind. She intended to live in that section of the city with a friend, perhaps another nurse, and help the sick in the neighborhood. She clarified that this way her neighbors would know her and feel more comfortable asking for help. It would be like bringing the clinics to the neighborhood residents, since most do not visit the clinics.

Mrs. Loeb was taken aback. No solicitor for funds had ever pitched this idea to her. Yet, she had a good feeling about Lillian. She is said to have reported to her daughter Nina, "I have had a wonderful experience. I have talked with a young woman who is either crazy or a genius."[2]

Lillian propositioned not only Mrs. Loeb but also her son-in-law Jacob Schiff, a well-known, hard-edged financier in the international banking world. Schiff was intrigued with the idea. He believed strongly in the Jewish concept of *tzdakah*, a religious duty to help the disadvantaged. He espoused several principles in his charitable giving. While he supported the organizations, he did not believe in bearing the full costs. He signed on partners, bought buildings, and "planted the seeds." He would say that "an individual should not be identified with any charity since the time might come when the institution would need larger funds and the public would not have been trained to support it."[3]

Her efforts paid off. Between the two, Wald and Brewster would be guaranteed $120 a month to cover living expenses and nursing supplies. He gave money not only to the organization but to Wald herself so that she could thrive. The agreement stipulated that they could request additional funds as needed. Feeling triumphant, the two young nurses set out to make their mark. What they were about to witness and learn would enlighten their entire generation.

The first order of business was finding suitable rooms in this new menacing neighborhood. They wanted the convenience of a bathroom, a rarity in that neighborhood. They soon learned that they were not the only ones with the idea of moving into the neighborhood they sought to serve. They met two young men, almost like their counterparts, who lived in the area. The two gentlemen, Charles Stover and Edward King were teaching history to immigrants at the Educational Alliance. That was a major center set up to teach immigrants English, about

US customs and ways, history, the arts, and other subjects. It aimed to integrate the immigrants into society.

One of the young men mentioned a place on Rivington Street where women pursuing similar goals were living. They called their house the College Settlement. He suggested that they might take in the two budding nurses until they found their own quarters.

Miss Wald and Miss Brewster were surprised. They hadn't realized that others were doing the same work. The young women of the College Settlement House invited them in. They explained what a "Settlement" was. The idea was to reside or "settle" in the neighborhood one was serving in order to learn about it and find ways of improving it. Unbeknownst to Lillian, in Chicago, Jane Addams was embarking on a similar mission. Jane Addams would one day become one of Lillian's closest friends.

One of the residents summarized her positon for the inquisitive young nurses. "We don't think God meant some people to be poor and others rich. And we don't think 'charity' is really noble. It does not relieve poverty; it's more likely to preserve it. And we don't think it should be preserved."[4] The young hosts invited Lillian and Mary to live there temporarily.

Suddenly, Wald was among like-minded individuals. The Settlement house workers also came from middle-class families and had chosen to live among the people they served. Wald's idea, it turns out, was not original. In fact, many residents of the Settlement house credited their idea to Toynbee Hall in England. That was created by Oxford and Cambridge students years prior to improve the worst London slums. Yet, Wald and Brewster's purpose was different from that of their colleagues. Whereas others were focused on education, their goals were on improving the health of the community members. Their concerns were more physical and immediate.

So they set out to work. They made their way through the streams of people, the seemingly endless pushcarts and through the hustle-

---

Jane Addams co-founded the first settlement in the US, Hull House in Chicago. She championed many of the same causes as Lillian Wald and her team including women's suffrage, worker rights, and protections for children. She is the matriarch of the social work profession. In 1931, she was the first US woman to receive the Nobel Peace Prize.

and-bustle. They approached their work not just as nurses, but as teachers of good health. When they visited a patient, they not only tried to cure him or her, but to teach him or her how to avoid becoming sick in the first place. They meticulously documented their work daily. Jacob Schiff insisted on that as a condition for funding. At first, he wanted mostly statistics: How many patients did they see? What were the ailments? Results?

Wald's first report in July 1893 outlined her activities. She did so succinctly and without sentiment. Her early reports read like bulletins:

"Started with the bottle of Boric acid and clean clothes to hunt the baby I had seen on the street yesterday," the report begins.

She also tried to track down a child she noticed was suffering from an eye condition. Lillian had asked his address. The challenge was to find a single resident in these many-roomed buildings. She made inquiries at various apartments until she found him. She described the apartment as having "terrible filth everywhere." The clogged sinks were odorous. Floors were "reeking."

She drew a connection between cleanliness and hygiene along with health. While she had first set out to simply cure the ill, she realized that the state of the home was a crucial part of the equation.

Another report mentioned the patients' names and their treatment:

"Visit and care of typhoid patient 182 Ludlow Street. Visit to 7 Hester Street where in rooms of Nathan Solomon found two children with measles. After much argument, succeeded in bathing these two patients and the sick baby. The first time in their experience, they insisted, where water and soap could be applied to anyone with measles before seven days."

After a while of providing "just the facts" to her funder, Wald started to convey the story behind the patients she saw. Her descriptions were vivid. Schiff was drawn in. He began asking about the state of particular patients. He was no longer the detached philanthropist. He felt personally invested in their success.

As Lillian tried to make inroad in the new neighborhood, she employed some techniques. One of her strategies was to meet the residents in all the apartments of a tenement. She sometimes got referrals from one apartment for another. She visited one family where the father was unemployed and rheumatic. His right hand was deformed. He was too discouraged to search for employment. The family was supported by the mother. She nursed her own baby and that of an orphan. She was

Nurse tending to a mother and her child in their Lower East Side tenement when healthcare was sparse and unaffordable. (Courtesy of the Visiting Nurse Service of New York Records, Archives & Special Collections, Health Sciences Library, Columbia University)

paid ten dollars per month for this care. But six dollars and fifty cents of that was for rent of the shabby two-room apartment. To supplement their income, they lived in just one room and rented out the other. She slept on the floor with her husband on a pile of rags.

Lillian wondered how landlords could get away with renting out houses in deplorable conditions. For starters, there was no accountability. Inspections by health officials were rare. Second, a lot of what she witnessed was not illegal. It was unethical. So while it was technically not breaking the law, it was still wrong. Third, most residents did not have the language or negotiating skills to complain. And, finally, if a tenant left a dwelling, there were scores more to take his or her place.

Lillian decided that though she could not control many of these factors, she could hold the building staff more accountable. She scolded the janitor for not keeping up the building. He promised to improve. She told him she would return frequently to make sure he was doing his job adequately.

Meanwhile, Nurse Mary Brewster, Miss Wald's partner in this venture, was finding similarly startling sites. In a rear tenement, she found the very thin figure of Mrs. Berg "lying on vermin-infested bed without sheets or pillow cases and suffering from a severe case of puerperal septicemia."

Miss Brewster inquired of the patient of her medical history. To her surprise, patient Mrs. Berg had been seen by a doctor and been given a prescription. But she could not afford to buy the medicine.

The young nurse learned that the doctor did not want to return to the apartment because Mrs. Berg could no longer afford to pay him. She promised Mrs. Berg that she would discuss this with the doctor. She paused and looked at her ragged patient. She told her not to worry and that they would "work out something together."

Miss Brewster investigated the matter and found out that the doctor had been charging seventy-five cents per visit, a high sum for the indigent family. She tracked down the doctor and asked about Mrs. Berg. She ensured her tone was non-accusatory. She did not want to antagonize the situation. The doctor seemed callous and disinterested in the patient. Mary did not let him get away with his behavior.

Later, he met Mary at Mrs. Berg's apartment. He said in a frustrated tone, "There's nothing more to be done. I have left a prescription and if she takes it, she'll improve."[5]

Mr. Berg spoke to Mary in the hallway and told her he could not afford the medicine.

An avid problem solver, Mary thought quickly. Though she was mild-mannered and focused on community healthcare matters, she displayed a sharp business sense.

She asked him how much one day's supply of fish costs? She offered to lend him the money. She handed over the five dollars and said, "Tomorrow, you can go back to work and leave Mrs. Berg to me. You can repay the loan when it is convenient."[6]

Later that night, back at the Settlement, Mary relayed the story of the Bergs and the lackadaisical doctor. Lillian, more quick-tempered than Mary, wanted to rush out that moment and tell that physician what she thought of him. But she did not. She admired Mary's creativity in problem solving. She wanted to emulate that quality. She thought of what she had learned at her school, the asylum, and even back home in Rochester, New York. She pondered on the best way to deal with uncaring or incompetent individuals and injustice.

The next morning, the two nurses returned to the Berg's apartment. A surprise awaited them. The doctor had returned to his patient. What caused him to change his mind? Mary would discover that the five dollars she gave Mr. Berg wound up in the doctor's pocket.

Lillian spoke with the doctor outside in the hallway. She was furious but tried to contain herself. "The fee you received this morning was lent to Mr. Berg by my colleague. It was meant to set him on his feet again at his peddler's trade."[7] She explained that the family is desperately poor and cannot afford the doctor's bill.

But the doctor was unapologetic. He said he needed to run his practice and earn money.

For the next week, part of each of Lillian's and Mary's day was devoted to the Bergs. They obtained food staples through the United Hebrew Charities, they cleaned the apartment, and saw that the children were adequately cared for.

Mr. Berg was back to fish peddling. But that also meant there was no one to watch the children. Mary explained the situation to Mr. Berg. She said she could not spend the full day at the apartment as so many other sick people who need her attention. She asked if now that he is working, if he can pay someone to stay at the home.

Mr. Berg performed a quick mental calculation. He could afford three dollars per week. That would not be enough. At least six dollars per week would be needed. So Mary agreed to use emergency funds to cover the extra three dollars.

The Bergs were one of many households needing urgent care. Many such families feared hospitals and would not take their sick family members to them. They did not understand that hospitals could often take better care of them than they could, despite their best efforts. Part of what Mary and Lillian had to teach was for patients not to be afraid of hospitals.

As Lillian came to know her new community and the needs of its residents, her reports to Mr. Schiff became more personal. Whereas earlier reports were clinical, now her reports contained patients' names and sometimes their situations. Mr. Schiff felt more an emotional connection to those whom he was funding. They were not anonymous patients.

One of Lillian's reports to Mr. Schiff read, "Elias Blumenthal living on the street is only fifteen years old. Mrs. Jacobson and her two children are homeless and without work." She told of residents that were too proud to accept handouts. In one episode, she relayed to Schiff that she had a friend pretend her son needed tutoring so that the family could "earn" money.[8]

She often narrated the plights of neighborhood residents and explained to him how her intervention benefited. In a November 1893 letter, for example, she mentions Mrs. Unterburgh was "successfully operated at the New York hospital but her husband, who had trouble with his eyes, was sent to a specialist for examination who reported paralysis of nerve and therefore hopeless."[9] She followed up with good news though. The city's allowance for the blind will allow him to start a candy store near one of the public schools.

She also spoke of her patients' fears of being outcasts or of being taken away to an asylum. "In a rear tenement, on the top floor on Allen Street, a doctor found a woman who was crazy and ill with pneumonia and typhoid being cared for by her fourteen-year-old daughter. She had been crazy for some time and the husband and child hid it fearing she would be forcibly taken to an asylum were it known." Wald later

Mother cooks in a Lower East Side tenement in 1910 with two children playing. (Courtesy of the Visiting Nurse Service of New York Records, Archives & Special Collections, Health Sciences Library, Columbia University.)

Hester Street vendors in Lower East Side in early 1890s around the time Lillian Wald and Mary Brewster moved to the neighborhood. (Courtesy of the Byron Company Collection at the Museum of the City of New York and the Visiting Nurse Service of New York Records, Archives & Special Collections, Health Sciences Library, Columbia University.)

added that the doctor "told us in time" so they were able to make her "human and decent."[10]

Her letters would go beyond describing patients' needs to offering a broader view of public health, at a time when that viewpoint was unusual. She knew about the healthcare community. "Nursing is only the beginning of what we have got to do here," Lillian would say.

Schiff answered Wald's letters with empathy, council, and wisdom. He wrote in one letter:

"I am almost afraid to think of the misery which surrounds us here on all sides, but I know you always feel as I do, and perhaps more so, that those whose lot it has become to help their unfortunate fellow beings are more to be envied than those who have a quiet and easy life and know nothing of the misfortune which exists in the world."

One night, Lillian found herself sleepless. The heat was oppressive. She stumbled across her tiny bedroom and looked out the window on the street. In the middle of the night, there were still crowds of people scattered along the sidewalks, sleeping and selling from the few pushcarts active that time of night. How different it was from the still of the night she was accustomed to uptown! And how very different from how she grew up in Rochester. As she observed children sleeping on the fire escapes, she felt overwhelmed by the enormity of her task.

So over the next few months, Lillian and Mary's work continued. They visited tenements transferring from one to the next on the rooftops. They pleaded for food for their patients from charities and their personal networks. They taught their patients about hygiene, cared for the sick, advocated for their employment, and made small loans where possible.

Chapter 4

First Years in the Lower East Side

Their timing was challenging. The year 1893 brought a severe financial panic. The country was sinking into an economic depression. Tenement residents sunk deeper into poverty. Factories decreased or ceased production. This meant they needed fewer workers. Hundreds suddenly became unemployed. In this period, there was no unemployment insurance. There were very few, if any, welfare benefits. Society had virtually no safety nets. Job losses were mounting. This was a double-edged sword. On the one hand, many jobs lost were dangerous, laborious, and exploitive. On the other hand, they provided at least some income.

Mary and Lillian brought on a third nurse to help. Two nurses they recruited resigned within days. The third candidate lasted. Even Mrs. Loeb's daughter, Nina, would come downtown to help with errands. She was curious about how her mother's recipients of funds were faring. Still, it was not nearly enough. A few nurses were powerless to relieve the suffering of thousands.

Always politically astute, Lillian knew she and her nurses needed an official badge to be taken seriously. It would lend them credibility. And so she sought a connection with civic authority. Through her network, she met the President of the Board of Health. She asked for an insignia. The official was supportive of her effort and sanctioned their wearing the badge engraved on its circle "Visiting Nurse, under the auspices of the Board of Health."

> The Panic of 1893 brought upon an economic depression. It started with a crash in wheat prices and was exacerbated by bank runs, whereby depositors withdraw their savings abruptly. A "credit crunch" ensued whereby it was difficult for households or firms to borrow money. As a result, about 15,000 firms and 500 financial institutions went bankrupt. Unemployment hovered near twenty percent.

As the now insignia-wearing young nurses took on more patients, they started to outgrow the Settlement house they were living in. They needed to set up in a place of their own. Their benefactor, Jacob Schiff, agreed.

By autumn, she and Mary Brewster moved to a walk-up apartment nearby at 27 Jefferson Street. The tenement apartment had a tiny bedroom, a small dining room, and a kitchen. It had a bathroom in the hallway, which was a very rare luxury in that neighborhood. Most tenements merely had facilities in the backyard, which contributed to hygiene and health problems in the community.

Lillian later recounted the objections she encountered for this move.

"Naturally, objections to two young women living alone in New York under these circumstances had to be met, and some assurance as to our material comfort was given to the anxious, though at heart sympathetic families, by compromising on good furniture, a Baltimore heater for cheer, and simple but adequate household appliances."[1]

In other words, the nurses did not want to have luxury in their apartment when the people they were serving had so little. Yet, their families insisted they have certain comforts. So they furnished the apartment from their families' contributions. They transformed the drab tenement into a home. They painted the grimy floors, made curtains, hung pictures on the cracked walls, and filled the apartment with plants. They furnished a sitting room with pictures, books, and restful chairs. The two shared the tiny bedroom. If the nurses were to use the bathroom in the hallway, they learned they had to rise early.

It was time to celebrate their new home. At last, they had their own place to take on their enormous tasks. They cooked a celebratory meal and invited Tommy McRae, the son of the building's janitress. After silently eating his meal, he left. Had Mary and Lillian offended him? Did they do something wrong?

Later that night, there was a knock on the door. It was Mrs. McRae, the janitress. She looked curiously at the new tenants and stepped into their apartment. "I have to take a look around up here. The way Tommy came crashing down the basement, I thought there must be a fire in the house. But no. It was just that he couldn't wait to tell me about the things he saw here and the lovely meal he had eaten. He said, 'Mother, them ladies live like the Queen of England.' You've fixed up the place for sure!"[2]

Lillian thanked Mrs. McRae and explained that they would be doing some of their work from the apartment. "We hope people in the neighborhood will come to call on us whenever they like, if they think we can be of any help to them, or if they'd just like to sit and rest awhile."

After learning they were nurses, Mrs. McRae proclaimed she would look after the two newcomers. She would protect them from neighbors visiting them at all hours. She said she would "watch the door like a hawk, and send off those that have no business botherin' ye."[3]

Mrs. McRae bestowed a loving and protective energy to the two young nurses. She was their mother away from home. Lillian later wrote about her, "From her basement home she was no small influence in holding us to sanity. Humor, astuteness, and sympathy were needed and she gave them in abundance."

She sometimes intervened to tell the nurses they needed to take care of themselves over the visitors. When the nurses returned home, Mrs. McRae would report on the happenings in the apartment during their absence.

"Lots of visitors tonight," she would report.

"Were messages left or names?" asked Lillian curiously.

"No, darlings, nothing at all. I know for sure they didn't bring you anything."[4]

Lillian and Mary usually left the apartment key with Ms. McRae. One day they forgot. Upon returning home, they opened the door to their apartment and found a surprise. A well-known "society woman" was sitting in their living room. Lillian and Mary exchanged glances. How could she have gotten there? Mrs. McRae explained that she had taken her up the fire escape! This was quite the adventure and certainly for a lady such as she.

"Perhaps, you could have had her wait in your apartment or had her return," Lillian said to Mrs. McRae.

"It's no harm at all. She'll be havin' lots of talk for her friends on this."[5]

Suddenly, the two nurses felt like true residents of the Lower East Side. And yet they were so different.

The other tenants were all Russian or Romanian Jews. Though Lillian was also Jewish, their worlds were far apart. Her ancestors were from a prosperous German Jewish family which had become rather assimilated to the US in the previous generation. Yet, these were recent immigrants. They were primarily fleeing from violent pogroms or attacks back in their home countries like Russia or Eastern European countries. They spoke little English, had few marketable skills and, importantly, severely lacked "street knowledge" of how their new nation worked. They did not know about hygiene and nutrition laws, how to find gainful employment, or how to navigate the country's complex systems. Some may have been learned in their home countries. Sadly, those studies were not valued in the new country.

Their predominant trade was garment manufacturing. Some immigrants had makeshift shops in the same places they lived. Often, as many as ten would cram in a small, humid tenement hunched over sewing machines. Pay was low, and the industry was highly competitive. Others were runners whereby they would deliver piles of fabric to various addresses. Others did not work at home. They worked in factories around the neighborhood. Hours were long, and conditions were very poor.

Besides coming from vastly different backgrounds, the two nurses faced another challenge: the patients' pride. Many were loath to accept charity. Nurses who proceeded them were usually connected with a church or charity work. Some patients objected to receiving "handouts." While some declined services out of pride, others were suspicious of receiving help from strangers. To counter this, Wald decided to charge for her services: ten cents per visit. This transformed the way patients

Early Settlement nurse crossing rooftops saving the trouble of going up and down the stairs. (Courtesy of the Visiting Nurse Service of New York Records, Archives & Special Collections, Health Sciences Library, Columbia University)

viewed their service. The caveat was that patients who could not afford to pay, did not have to. They were encouraged to think of it as "neighborly service" rather than the distant hand of charity.

Sometimes, they bartered. They helped a Russian man's wife with medical care. He would not accept any handouts and wanted to pay them. But he had no funds. So, the nurses asked if he could use his carpentry skills and build them a storage shelf unit.

When the shelves were completed, Lillian stopped at his house. "That's exactly what we wanted. And they are beautifully made. I'm afraid we didn't agree on a fee ahead of time. I hope this amount is acceptable to you." She put money on the table.

"Oh no! No, lady. Please. Was for you. To show my appreciation."[6]

Lillian was torn. She knew he was hungry and desperately needed the money. But his pride interfered. She took back the money, at his request.

Yet, not all neighbors were ethical. Some who heard of the charitable donations would make up their circumstances to try to "get in on the free stuff." Usually, the nurses gave out loans though rather than gifts, and most were paid back.

Family in a Lower East Side tenement in 1910 in photo taken by Jacob Riis. (Courtesy of the Jacob Riis Collection at the Museum of the City of New York and the Visiting Nurse Service of New York Records, Archives & Special Collections, Health Sciences Library, Columbia University.)

Others struggled with the conflict between their religious beliefs and the demand of their jobs. Religious Jews do not work on Saturdays, which is their Sabbath or Shabbat. Yet, many jobs required that. In fact, there were some signs which read: "If you do not come for work on Saturday, do not bother coming on Monday."

Yet there were times when people put their religious beliefs and customs behind them to help their neighbors. Lillian recounts when an Orthodox Jewish father on the Sabbath (Friday night to Saturday night) took one of the lights from the table to show her the way down five flights of dark tenement stairs. Handling fire on the Sabbath is prohibited.

Lillian protested that the man should not break his Sabbath rules by carrying light. He protested. He whispered, "It is no sin for me to handle a light on the Sabbath to show respect to a friend who has helped to keep a family together."[7]

Though some in their new neighborhood took to them, many in the medical profession did not. Many physicians serving the area felt threatened. They had earned their living treating patients here, and now these two nurses were providing services for free or for below market rate. Some doctors were said not to treat patients until they were paid first. Yet, Wald and Brewster tried to regain their patients' trust.

Then, there were tragedies that Lillian and her team were powerless to stop. She was moved by the story of twenty-one-year-old carpenter, Samuel, and Ida, his bride. They were young sweethearts in Poland and immigrated to America for a better life. Or so they thought.

One day, Samuel knocked on the nurses' door in a panic. Lillian knew at once something was gravely wrong. She followed him to the top floor of his tenement building. She opened the door. She saw immediately that his beloved wife, Ida, was dying. The midwife was in the corner of the room. She was trying to deliver the baby. She looked frightened.

"No one could have done any better," she insisted, "not any doctor."

She paused and looked down. Trembling, she said she had called for a doctor. Yet, he had left Ida lacerated and agonizing in pain because the expected fee had been paid only in part.

With the family's resources depleted, the only option was to send Ida to the city hospital. Samuel rode in the ambulance and watched over his dying wife. Sadly, a few hours later, she and the baby died.

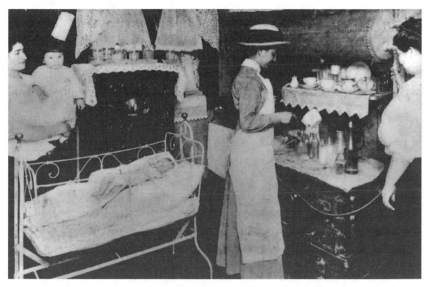

Early Visiting Nurse Service staff member caring for a mother and her ill baby. (Courtesy of the Henry Street Settlement.)

For Lillian, this was a wake-up call. She realized that some doctors would only perform services for money. If their patients could not pay for all the services, that was their problem. She knew that reforms were needed. And so was accountability. That doctor, she thought, should not be allowed to get away with walking away from a patient who could not afford services. She tried to get him reprimanded. Yet, her calls for change fell largely on deaf ears.

Chapter 5

Visiting Nurse Service at the Henry Street Settlement

Over the coming months, their team grew by taking on new nurses. They called themselves the Visiting Nurse Service. Cases flew through their door. The newly named organization treated 125 people and counseled the many who came knocking on their doors. The Panic of 1893 continued to hinder the economy causing more unemployment and poverty. Wald and her team were needed more than ever.

Wald later recalled the interaction with neighbors seeking their services: "In the early morning, before we had time to put the kettle on, people began their tramp up our five flights. The procession continued after our nursing rounds were ended until the last minute of the night, before we sank into fatigued sleep. They came begging us to help them find work, or at least to give them a ticket entitling them to a few days of the 'made work' which was being provided as a relief measure."

They also tried to be solid stewards of resources. The following is a monthly itemization showing their record-keeping detail:

Eggs for Mrs. Boardman	$.25
Two prescriptions for Mrs. Stein	$.40
Milk bill for Lee-Lo Sing	$.30
Carfare	$.20
Beech baby at day nursery	$.90
Mrs. Schiller's medicine	$.20
Fixing Mr. Lipschitz's spectacles	$.18
To Mr. Klein to buy coal to sell	$1.00

The itemized list shows that money was spent with small expenses of food, medicine, and other needs for patients.[1] Neighbors reached out for help in advocating on their behalf at schools and other institutions. One patient asked for help for her son, Louis.

"Louis is bad," she cried. "He won't cure his head, and they won't let him in school as long as his head is sore. Look at him—such a big boy and can't read. It's bad enough we can't read—we wanted our son to know how."

She spoke with Louis who said he wanted to go to school. He explained, "Every time I go to school, the teacher tells me to go home."[2]

Lillian inquired whether he had taken medicine. He had many times. She paused in thought. She thought she had figured out the problem. Often, medications required that patients were able to read the label. Likely, he could not read it and therefore was not applying it correctly.

She applied the ointment prescribed to his head. She made arrangements to check up regularly on his progress. The medication, once applied properly, worked. Louis happily returned to school that fall.

His case was solved. But the larger issue was still wrong. Lillian realized that there were many children in Louis's position. Many were prevented from going to school for similar reasons just as he had been. She knew she would have to push hard for significant changes in schools.

She felt she could only partly blame the teachers and schools. They were, she reflected, part of a larger, broken system. She knew that the classes were overcrowded, often with as many as sixty pupils in a single room and often three children on a seat. Though it is hard to imagine today, no schools had doctors or nurses on their premises during this time. This was something Lillian Wald and her colleagues would change.

Though the Visiting Nurse Service was focused on medical care, the economic landscape they were working in was shifting rapidly. They could not ignore it. The Panic of 1893 and the subsequent economic fallout was worsening. Workers were beginning to organize more strikes. Calls for safer worker conditions, which fell largely on deaf ears, were growing louder. Poverty and unemployment were growing worse. Thus, Wald's organization began to attract not just health care professionals but also social reformers. Whether she liked it or not, Wald was entering the heated social reform movement.

The expanding nurse service needed a larger space. They had outgrown their apartment. Neighbors came by day and night for help. The janitress Mrs. McRae would yell from the basement trying to control the traffic and ensure the two nurses received proper rest. She would tell them, "I know what I'm doing. You look after everyone else. Somebody's got to look after you."

Wald petitioned to her philanthropist Mr. Schiff. He agreed and the search for a suitable house began. After an exhaustive search, the nurses ended up at 265 Henry Street next to the house where Lillian

Children around a table making flowers by hand in a Lower East Side tenement in 1910. (Courtesy of the Jacob Riis Collection at the Museum of the City of New York and the Visiting Nurse Service of New York Records, Archives & Special Collections, Health Sciences Library, Columbia University.)

had taught the first hygiene class in. Mr. Schiff purchased the house. As they moved in during 1895, this would serve as the headquarters for the Visiting Nurse Service and as a residence for several of the nurses. It survives to this day as a social services site recognized worldwide.

The red brick Georgian style building harked back to earlier days in the neighborhood when it was more serene. As difficult it would have been for Wald to imagine given how much the surroundings changed, the three story red-brick house stood on what was the Henry Rutgers farm.

Though the neighborhood profoundly changed, the house curiously did not. Surrounded by tenements, the "house on Henry Street" they moved into retained its character. Like a metaphor for the Visiting Nurse Service's vision and beacon of light for the community, the resident nurses could look out the window each evening into the sunset illuminating the neighborhood. It had what one nurse called "a quiet dignity" in all the noise and bustle of a city's slum area. It had a promise of stability for the future.

The neighborhood also had echoes of its past. Wald would regale

Merchants and peddlers selling goods on the Lower East Side. (Courtesy of the Visiting Nurse Service of New York Records, Archives & Special Collections, Health Sciences Library, Columbia University.)

visitors with historic snippets. She would note that Nathan Hale, a Yale college student around the time of the American Revolution, was said to have been hanged by the British in a nearby orchard. Hale was suspected of being a spy for the American colonists. A nearby church still had a slave gallery, as slaves were not freed completely in New York City until 1827.

And they received a new neighbor. It was the janitress from Lillian's and Mary's old flat. She moved her family to live near the young nurses. She gave up her rent-free apartment in order to care for them longer than the two years they were in the Jefferson Street apartment. She was like their mother in the neighborhood. As the nurses watched over the neighborhood, she watched over them.

With the expanded space, Wald increased her staff. The Visiting Nurse Service began to develop a reputation not only in the community but also amongst nurses and nursing students. One new nurse would become one of Wald's closest friends.

Her name was Lavinia Dock, who was described by a colleague as a "small, short, sort of roly poly little person with curly hair." The pioneering Lillian Wald had met her match in the precocious and irreverent, yet politically passionate Lavinia Dock. Like Lillian, she came from a middle-class family and private school education. Her work was focused on disaster relief such as aiding the victims of the historic Johnstown Flood. She also authored one of the first nursing textbooks.

She was more politically minded than the more practical Lillian Wald. Her attention was focused on women's rights. She firmly believed that it would be difficult to make needed changes in society without giving women the right to vote. She noted the effect living at Henry Street had on her. "It was at Henry Street that I really began to think. I had the privilege of working with Lillian Wald, a social genius, the one with the gift for bringing people and opportunities together."

Lavinia's language was blunt. She was determined for nurses to command respect and wanted to improve the training and educational requirements for the field. She felt physicians stood in her way.

To one doctor, she wrote: "It seems to me particularly unseemly and ungrateful for physicians to talk about 'fighting' nurses. Why, you owe 70 percent of your success and prestige to nurses. And here you are trying to beat down the very women on whom your success depends. If you do not think that is shabby, I do." Dock then called doctors "selfish and stupid for failing to recognize what was in their own best interests."[3]

About fifteen nurses joined the organization. They were educated, middle class, and unmarried. They became the "Henry Street family." They understood their common goals and provided each other emotional support. Without the burdens of husbands and children, they gave their energies totally to their work.

Each day had a familiar schedule. At 7:30 a.m., Lillian would meet with her staff at the breakfast table and discuss the day's requests from needy patients and physicians. A request may be, "Show me how to care for my firstborn baby." After breakfast, the nurses began their work. They dressed in what became recognizable in the community as a Visiting Nurse—blue uniforms with matching hats carrying black bags. They often moved between apartments by stepping from the rooftop of one tenement building to another. It saved the trouble of running up and down the long-winded stairs.

Under Wald's guidance, nurses did not simply treat the symptoms of patients. Just as she had set out to do with Mary Brewster, she saw to it that these nurses were to understand the root causes of their patients' ailments. Was their nutrition adequate? Was the family earning enough

Ad for Visiting Nurse Service in mid-1920s offering $1 visits in any of its locations. (Courtesy of the Visiting Nurse Service of New York Records, Archives & Special Collections, Health Sciences Library, Columbia University.)

money? If not, why not? What was the sanitation level of the dwelling, and how could it be improved? What was the mental and emotional stress of the family? Once nurses identified the causes, they were then to educate the families on how to improve their conditions. Above all, the Visiting Nurse Service strove to see the patient as a person not just one who needs medical attention.

Some of the nurses went a step further. They tried solving the problems for their patients. Some recommended jobs for unemployed husbands or looked into a police record. Some also paid for food and rent from their own pockets.

They were providing more than services. They were reforming healthcare. The Visiting Nurse Service became guardians of public health. For most of their patients, it was the first time in their lives they had public healthcare. It was said that Wald was referred to as the "Angel of Henry Street."

Lillian's old life in Rochester would sometimes merge with that of her current life as a nurse on the Lower East Side. Her family from

In this dining room at the Henry Street Settlement, the organization that would become the National Association for the Advancement of Colored People (NAACP) was born. (Photograph by Paul Kaplan.)

Rochester came to visit. It was eye-opening for them. Her niece, Harriet, would visit the Henry Street Settlement House and dine with the staff. Harriet would catch a glimpse of a world she had never seen nor scarcely heard about outside its doors. Lillian's mother, Mrs. Minnie Wald, came to live there for a period as well. Lillian put her up in her own room and encouraged her to interact with the staff and with the boys and girls who came in. She taught embroidery classes and read the children stories. She was well-liked in the house.

Lillian wrote a letter to her Uncle Sam about her mother, "My mother is remarkable for her age. Though she is not easy to manage, the children all love her and she is young in heart and young in speech too. In fact, I do not think that she has changed at all."

Over the next few years, the staff multiplied. Lillian still referred to resident staff as "her family." Lay workers and non-nurse staff joined as well. So did Nina Loeb, the once skeptical daughter of Betty Loeb who had initially funded Wald's request when it seemed like a faint dream. Eventually, there were also a few male residents.

Lillian ensured the necessary values were part of the selection for new nurses. She sought those not only with technical competence but those who had a heart for those whom they were administering medical care. They could find fault with the system but not loathe the people themselves.

As the Settlement expanded, so did its need for money. About half of its income came from nurses fees. While some patients could not afford services, others paid. There was the occasional contribution from those in the neighborhood. One wrote, "I see in the papers that you need money. You took care of my little boy when he was so bad burned and all my life since then I pray God, make me rich so I can help you big. But he hasn't answered my prayer so I send you this which I know isn't much but it's all I have." The letter was accompanied by a ten dollar bill.

Yet, these revenues were not enough to meet the growing expenses. The remainder came from continued support of Jacob Schiff and his mother-in-law in addition to "friends of friends in the German-Jewish community." Schiff's contributions, while generous and plentiful, were limited in that he supported many other charities which competed for his dollars. He gave ten percent of his income to charity and urged others to do so as well. Over the years, Lillian's friendship with him grew. So did their trust. By this time, she was filing yearly—rather than time-consuming monthly—reports. They often shared meals together at his grand residence on Fifth Avenue or at the Settlement. He wrote to her in 1905 expressing his warmth and gratitude for their friendship. "If we are beloved by you so are you by us and if you say, our friendship does mean something to you, so have we become more imbued with the spirit of responsibility wealth should impose upon those to whom it is given by Providence."[4] In other words, he thanked Lillian for keeping him grateful for his riches and accountable for giving away a percentage to compelling causes like the Settlement.

As electricity lit up the nation, Schiff contributed money to the Settlement for it too to be "lit up." He gave money for community centers. He introduced her to other philanthropists. He coached her on how to approach and nurture relationships with the wealthy.

Lillian was artful when seeking donations. A *New Yorker* article described how she would never ask directly for money but would describe the abject needs. Philanthropists felt compelled to give. "Socially she is much in demand among the possessors of great wealth, and she is often at their houses, friendly, magnetic, disarming. She leaves them, if not endorsing her view of life, at least magnanimously admitting that there is much to be said on both sides. She never asks for

Henry Street Settlement nurse in horse-drawn carriage in the then rural Bronx of New York in 1906. The organization was branching out to many locations. (Courtesy of the Visiting Nurse Service of New York Records, Archives & Special Collections, Health Sciences Library, Columbia University.)

money. Instead, with an embroidery of telling anecdotes, she describes the need for more nurses. Or she depicts the pitiful straits of children without playgrounds."[5] One philanthropist remarked, "It costs $5,000 to sit next to her at dinner" referring to her persuasive ways of asking for sizable donations.

She wrote to Mr. Schiff about one new recruit. "The best thing I can say of her sympathy and understanding is that she has never returned after visiting the most wretched with an expression of disgust for the people, but very much pity for their poverty and their ignorance. That seems good material for a start."

But Schiff expressed concerns about the direction the Settlement may have been taking. He questioned whether new recruits were genuinely interested in the mission or were just there for the experience. He wrote,

"It is not at all unlikely that some of the earnest young ladies who now come to the Settlement to work in it and with it, are to some extent attracted to it 'just because it is a family.' Yet a society, even if this feature is kept in the background, would be less of an attraction to

Kids play outside near the Henry Street Settlement. The need for a playground was apparent. (Courtesy of the Henry Street Settlement)

many a young woman who would otherwise like to engage in the great work which unites you and other members 'of the family.'"[6]

Heeding his advice, Lillian tweaked her recruiting process. Like Miss Sutliffe who had once interviewed her and been on the lookout for candidates with a passing interest, Lillian added rigor to the recruiting process. She also avoided young women with a "martyr complex." They wanted to give of themselves but it did not understand or care for its day-to-day realities.

The Settlement also began a new function. Lillian saw that the visiting nurses could provide valuable services for insurance companies. By making their customers healthier, it could only help the insurance companies save on future healthcare cost payouts.

Her vision coincided with Metropolitan Life Insurance's new philosophy. In 1909, Vice President of Metropolitan Life Haley Fiske announced that the company was "not merely a business proposition but a social program." To enact this, he hired the social worker Lee Frankel. He envisioned insurance as a "powerful means toward improving the lot of the underprivileged."[7] He created the company's Welfare Division.

This had powerful implications for the Settlement's clients. If some had insurance, much of their healthcare costs would paid. Suddenly, it would be affordable. Insurance could also help educated policyholders about ways to keep healthy.

This was especially needed in this period with the severe outbreak of tuberculosis. It was sometimes referred to as the "white plague" and was responsible for a staggering 1 out of 5 death claims. Joining the Settlement in educating patients, Metropolitan Life had its 10,000 agents deliver a pamphlet called "A War on Consumption" to millions.

Soon after, the partnership was formalized between the Metropolitan Life Company and the Henry Street Settlement's Visiting Nurse Service. Lillian Wald had challenged the company to "insure

---

Tuberculosis is an infectious disease that has been present in humans since ancient times. During the nineteenth and early twentieth century, it affected a significant percentage of the population. It was known as "consumption" due to the weight loss associated with it. Public awareness posters encouraging preventing the disease were prevalent. One ad read "Careless spitting, coughing, sneezing spread influenza and tuberculosis."

As their work expanded to new areas in later decades, the Henry Street Settlement Visiting Nurse Service drove its own cars to attend to patients. (Courtesy of the Visiting Nurse Service of New York Records, Archives & Special Collections, Health Sciences Library, Columbia University.)

America'sxworkers with a larger humanitarian perspective." The resulting program mobilized Henry Street Settlement nurses to visit very ill industrial policy holders.

It began as a three month experiment on Manhattan's West Side. Later, it was extended throughout all of New York City. Insurance agents encouraged their policyholders to report illnesses. Agents distributed cards with the closest visiting nurse. Many received treatment for illnesses like smallpox, tuberculosis, influenza, and diphtheria.[8]

The program was a success. Later, it expanded to thirteen other cities. Though the Henry Street Settlement's Visiting Nurse Service was not yet in these cities, Metropolitan Life partnered with other healthcare social service agencies. This partnership was the largest endeavor launched at the time. Soon after, other insurance companies followed like John Hancock Insurance.

In her autobiography, *The House on Henry Street,* Lillian explained the great impact of the program. "The company thereby gave an enormous impetus to education and hygiene in the homes and treatment of the sick on the only basis that makes it possible for persons of small means to receive nursing without charity—namely, through insurance."[9]

Years later, after film and radio were prevalent, she lauded the company's attempts to reach the masses through these new mediums. Throughout this expansion of services, the Settlement tried to build its internal community. More than anything, the Henry Street Settlement became a home for its workers. It was not just a job. Staff had meals, slept, and socialized in the house. It was a community within a community. Like the dinners at the College Settlement where Lillian had stayed years before, the dinner discussions were dynamic.

A young graduate student appeared at the House one day. He wanted to gain "real world experience" to complement his studies. Lillian looked at him curiously and wondered how he could be of service. She asked him if he embroidered.

Lillian was not being sarcastic. She noticed that many women had beautiful embroidery patterns. They learned them in their native countries. It was a source of their pride. Yet, many in their new communities were indifferent to them. Lillian's idea was to showcase their embroideries at the House or at galleries coupled with lectures on the various styles, patterns and techniques.

The graduate student came alive with an idea. He suggested organizing a baseball team like the Ludlow Street Leopards versus the Grand Street Giants. Lillian smiled as she noted that her team was seeking a baseball expert "particularly one with a little imagination."

Yet the Visiting Nurse Service was not without tragedy. Mary Brewster, the co-founder and co-pioneer of the organization's early days, was quite ill. She was quite sick before the move to Henry Street. But she recovered sufficiently to stay in the new house. Yet, soon after, her illness returned and she died. The one who sought to improve the health of hundreds fell victim to illness herself and died young. Lillian was deeply saddened.

The janitress Mrs. McRae who had watch over Lillian and Mary when they were on Jefferson Street and again on Henry Street fell ill. When her end was near, Lillian also had a very sick family member who needed her. She was torn. She did not want to leave the City when Mrs. McRae was so ill. Yet, Mrs. McRae advised her, "Darlin' you ought to go. You go. I promise not to die until you come back." She kept her promise.[10]

Chapter 6

Advocate for Children

With the Visiting Nurse Services blossoming, Lillian turned her attention to children. She realized that they needed a safe place to play. Many were getting injured by wagons and carriages while playing in highly trafficked streets. Parents were complaining. She witnessed children at their outdoor games dodging pushcarts and vehicles.

Her solution was to open a playground by combining the Henry Street Settlement's backyard with adjacent ones. Her original plan was to use this space for "cripples, chronic invalids, and convalescents," but changed her mind after realizing the need for a safe place for children to play. The playground was an immediate hit in the neighborhood.

She sought public playgrounds also so children could have space to play. She attributed some of their lack of discipline to this lack of space. "There's so little for them to do outside of school hours, except to stand around on corners and of course occasionally get into trouble just for the excitement of it. But if there were playgrounds . . ."

She was often met with resistance. Common culprits were budgets, bureaucracy, and regulations. A school official pushed back. They said they could not open the school at all hours and leave the children unsupervised.

Lillian offered an experiment to show its value. She said her staff would be glad to volunteer as inspectors to find the most effective ways of using the playground. Once they made their case for its importance to the School Board, she figured they would use their own staff for the necessary supervision.

Her efforts to convince administrators at public schools to have their grounds stay open after school and during summers to serve as recreation centers was ultimately successful. Her argument that it was valuable wasted space was compelling. It took time but by 1898, three years after the establishment of the Henry Street House with its own playground, designated New York City schools were opened as recreational centers.

She became a public figure for children's rights. She mobilized a petition campaign for the famed Metropolitan Museum of Art to remain open on Sundays so workers and their children could have access. Otherwise, the institution was in practical use only for the affluent who could afford to take off from work to visit during the week.

In *The House on Henry Street,* she explains how this lack of oversight of museum hours exposes a larger problem within the City. "The woeful lack of imagination displayed in building a city without recognizing the need of its citizens for recreation through play, music, and art, has been borne in upon us many times."[1]

The petition to keep the famed museum open on Sundays was successful. The museum was willing to try it. They reported mixed success. On the one hand, they report that the attendance on Sunday was "respectable, law-abiding, and intelligent" with the laboring classes well represented. On the other hand, the Museum was obliged to report that the Sunday opening had "offended some of the Museum's best friends and supporters leading to a loss in the bequest of $50,000."[2]

In thinking about how to expand opportunities for the children of the Lower East Side, she came up with a novel idea. She would have wealthy supporters open their country homes to neighborhood children. Children who had never been outside a dense urban environment would get to spend at least a little time in nature. No longer would they be cut off from seeing plants, flowers, and knowing where the food they ate came from. She sympathized with their need to see "real things." She recalled how living exclusively in a dense urban environment colored their thinking. One child believed that the buffalo he saw on his first visit to the zoo was the butterfly in his storybook. Another mistook a crocodile for a field mouse. The program started as day trips which evolved into summer week-long trips. Finally, the Henry Street camps were born. Friends of the Henry Street Settlement bequeathed their estates to the organization for this purpose.

One boy who was part of the excursions to the summer camp later became a major donor of the Settlement. He explained his reasons for the gift. "The Henry Street Settlement House took me and a lot of Irish and Italian kids and sent us off to the country. You can't explain what a thrill it was. I'll never forget it. There's no way I can really pay them back. I never knew what a cow was."[3]

Boys from Henry Street Settlement enjoying the outdoors on the Warburg Estate. This was part of programming to help urban children experience the countryside. (Courtesy of the Visiting Nurse Service of New York Records, Archives & Special Collections, Health Sciences Library, Columbia University.)

Boys on the way to camp with a Henry Street Settlement program to encourage urban youth to experience the outdoors. (Courtesy of the Visiting Nurse Service of New York Records, Archives & Special Collections, Health Sciences Library, Columbia University.)

Wald also made reforms in schools. She urged special classes for children with learning disabilities. By 1900, the Board of Education approved the first multi-age classroom for physically handicapped students and those with learning disabilities.

This was also a break-through. Until this point, students with either physical or mental disabilities rarely received customized education. As a result, many felt far behind. Dropout rates for this group soared. Many were left with no skills. Some resorted to street crime to survive. Yet, now there was an awareness that this group was not comprised of "troublemakers." Educators began to understand that some legitimately needed extra attention.

Parents often stood in the way of their children's progress. She was surprised how many parents in the Lower East Side regarded education as charity. She recounted a child who appeared at the Settlement one day for treatment for a minor injury. The nurses discovered that his hair was crawling with lice.

"Didn't your schoolteacher send word to your mother about this?" inquired the nurse.

"I never been to school," replied the child.[+]

A Settlement nurse visited the child's apartment. She saw an entire family in a basement, airless room hunched over sewing machines making garments. The mother admitted that none of her children had ever been to school.

She said with a tone of defiance. "Already I take charity from relief society. If children don't work, I have to ask for more. I don't take charity I don't need. My children and I earn all we can." There was an air of indignation to her voice coupled with fatigue.

This was the kind of "pride" some wanted to respect. If the parents wanted the family to earn more through their children working, who was the government or any social reformer to stop them, they reasoned.

Yet, for Lillian Wald and many other reformers, this missed the point. This was a false pride. And it harmed not only children but society in the long run for producing less educated children caught in the cycle of poverty.

She also convinced public schools to hire a public school nurse. She knew that diseases were being spread in the classroom. She aimed to convince the School Board that a nurse in school could relieve the spreading of disease. To prove the value of having a school nurse and to justify having the position be paid by the Board of Education, she devised a clever program. Her technique was to experiment with a few schools having a nurse and to show its success. She chose four schools which had high rate of excluding students due to medical reasons. Lillian then offered to pay half the salary of one of her nurses at the Settlement if the Board of Education paid the remaining half. The Board agreed. So a routine was set. A physician sent students needing medical attention to the school nurse.

Often, symbols were used in place of disease's full names to prevent embarrassment for the students. Usually, the children needed only disinfectant treatment of the eyes or an anti-bacterial ointment. Yet, other times, the symptoms were more serious. In that case, the nurse involved the parent. If no one at home could be reached or was available to take the child to the drug store, the nurse stepped in.

After a month, the trial was proving successful. The addition of a school nurse prevented disease breakouts and increased classroom attendance. The plan worked. So the Board voted on $30,000 for the employment of school nurses. Soon after, school districts around the nation followed. Later that year it was shown that schools with a nurse yielded superior attendance and healthier children. Eventually, schools routinely employed nurses.

She also fought for free school lunches. As many children were undernourished, their learning abilities were impaired. She asked, "Why the fuss over such a program?" when confronted by bureaucratic administrators. She noted that students who may appear mentally defective were actually just hungry. Along with public school nurses, free or subsidized lunches were introduced into the public school system.

In a 1905 letter to a city official, she outlined the reason children go hungry to school and how to fix it. "Many mothers leave home to go to work at such hours that they neither prepare breakfast for the children nor see them eat it, which is almost as important." She outlined the "foul and stuffy air" where often "five children sleep in one bed."

She further connected the lack of nutrition to the spread of tuberculosis.

Children in a Lower East Side tenement. (Courtesy of the Henry Street Settlement.)

"Tuberculosis also finds many victims among young people who might well have escaped infection if they had been properly fed."[5]

With these advances achieved, Lillian had reached yet a new revelation. It was important to nurture people's artistic talent and cultural backgrounds. Tending to their medical care was not enough. It only answered for their physical needs. Though it sounds cliché in present days, it was very unusual to express the importance of nurturing one's talents. The Visiting Nurse Service at the Henry Street Settlement would promote not only the survival of those they served but find ways for them to thrive.

With this goal in mind, the Henry Street Settlement took on social functions where clubs were formed for all ages. Kids were organized into sports teams. Others pursued art like drawing, music, or drama. In fact, the Neighborhood Playhouse on Grand Street, built in 1915, was a gift to the Settlement from two former volunteers, Alice and Irene Lewisohn, to provide a space for drama. The Playhouse would become an unlikely meeting between famous actors, directors, and the neediest of the neighborhood.

Contemporary dancers prepare for a performance at the Grand Street Playhouse. (Courtesy of the Henry Street Settlement.)

Benefactors Alice and Irene Lewisohn came to the Henry Street Settlement as young girls. They served as apprentices of the arts at the Settlement. Soon, they began to "originate art forms through new combinations of the elements of the drama and of pageantry."[6] The staff responded by offering classes in dance, pantomime and choral singing. Others studied costume making, props, and scenery. Ultimately, this expanded beyond what the Henry Street Settlement could offer in their space. So Alice and Irene Lewisohn in their later years opened the Neighborhood Playhouse.

At first, the Playhouse showed plays cast with amateur actors. But it became clear that professional actors were needed. Their specialized training and experience would bring up the shows' caliber and draw in audiences. At the same time, neighborhood amateur actors were needed given the purpose of the Henry Street Settlement. So the two worked side-by-side in productions. John Galsworthy, a noted English novelist and playwright, remarked that the Neighborhood Playhouse was where "magic had come to stay."[7]

In *The House on Henry Street*, Lillian summarized her intentions for the Playhouse. "It is my hope that the playhouse, identified with the neighborhood, may recapture and hold something of the poetry and idealism that belong to its people and open the door of opportunity for messages in drama and picture and song and story."[8]

Besides the arts, the Settlement also concentrated on teaching English. Classes were given or offered at the nearby Educational Alliance. Importantly, classes were integrated across races, ethnicities and national origin. It also provided a place for study. Tenements were too crowded for even the most ambitious of students to study. One boy complained, "I can never study at home because sister is always using the table to wash the dishes." This is why the Settlement opened study rooms for boys and girls to "find a quiet and restful place in which to do their work and receive coaching."[9]

The study rooms also doubled as a library. On Fridays, it was

---

The Grand Street Playhouse would become the venue for some of the most acclaimed artistic productions in the US. In 1938, the Playhouse staged famed Aaron Copland's opera *The Second Hurricane* directed by noted director Orson Welles. In the 1940s, it became known for its abstract dance theater, which the Playhouse director defined as "the art of motion which becomes the message as the medium."

Grand Street Playhouse in its early days where it was said "magic had come to stay." (Courtesy of the Henry Street Settlement.)

reserved for very young readers. Soon, the library took on a mission beyond New York. Attending the Southern Educational Conference, she was stirred by the story of a Southern minister. He told of poor white natives traveling miles over mountains to hear books read. His neighbors had no access to books of any kind. When she returned to the Settlement and told his story, the children immediately voted to send the minister some of the library's books. For two years, the Settlement's clubs purchased one book each month for them. After two years, the minister wrote that he finally had enough books to form something of a library. Besides books, the Settlement also offered free lunches at the Settlement house so children could experience a rare elegant meal.

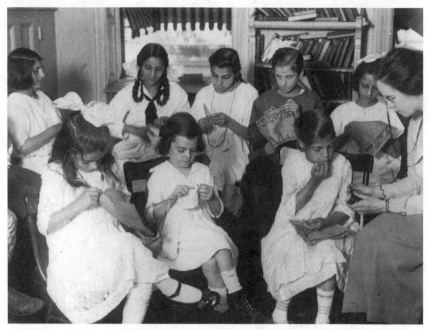

Girls learn to sew at the Henry Street Settlement. (Courtesy of the Henry Street Settlement.)

Models ride horse-drawn carriage with poster for the Henry Street Settlement. This was part of a public awareness campaign. (Courtesy of the Visiting Nurse Service of New York Records, Archives & Special Collections, Health Sciences Library, Columbia University.)

The Settlement had a lighter side too. Clubs that met at the House offered picnics and parties. Music was often played. Ethnic groups sometimes performed their native dances. Czechs and Russians, in particular, showcased their footwork. Menus at parties reflected the nationalities present.

Underlying the amusement of these gatherings was the tension between various ethnic groups. Some harbored resentment from their countries of origin. So the Settlement house served as a place for groups of various ethnicities to celebrate their cultures and learn about those of others. Lillian wrote her thoughts of why discriminations existed. She surmised that the root was people's lack of imagination. They could not imagine themselves in the positon or plight of others. In other words, they could not put themselves in another's shoes. Part of her work was to "stir these imaginations."

Chapter 7

The Social Reformer

Lillian Wald and her Visiting Nurse Service believed that the nation's future lay in the success of children. Today, it sounds trite. Yet that was an unusual philosophy at the time. The odds stacked against immigrant children were numerous.

Court records from the turn of the 20th century showed that recent immigrants' children outnumbered the native born in court cases by three and a half to one because "home life was so unbearable." Many parents sent their kids to work often in highly exploitive conditions. Many started work at aged six or seven often in a single room including their parents doing factory work. Lillian wrote that many "lost their childhoods in labor, working half the night, breathing foul air in windowless rooms, eating rotting food."[1] Worse still, the sick were often working and thought to have been spreading their diseases to other communities.

Some parents did not object to child labor. They saw their children as a source of financial support. This was a pervasive attitude in many of their native countries. There were some children who worked in textile mills about ten to twelve hours a day, six days a week breathing in poisoned dust.

Some older children also took a stance by participating in labor strikes. Union organizer Mary Harris Jones, known as "Mother Jones," led a "March of the Mill Children" from the Pennsylvania mills to the summer home of President Theodore Roosevelt in nearby Long Island, New York. Little boys injured by factory machines participated in the protests.

The time for social and labor reforms had come. The Visiting Nurse Service supported these child reform efforts. With pressure applied, New York adopted its first substantial law establishing limitations on child labor. But the laws could not be enforced. Not enough inspections were done to identify the organizations breaking the law. So little changed. But public sympathy was aroused.

"Mother Jones" was the nickname for Mary Harris Jones, an Irish-born dressmaker and teacher. A formidable part of the labor movement, she cofounded Industrial Workers of the World and helped pull off major strikes most notably among miners. Mine owners called her "the most dangerous woman in America" in 1902 for her success in organizing mine labor. Today, there is a magazine named for her.

Lillian knew that she had to win over the public for these causes. But how? She and her coworkers realized that they had to make this issue about the self-interest of the public. By talking about the contagious diseases and unsanitary work conditions of clothing producers, it would worry those who were purchasing and ultimately wearing the clothes or smoking the cigarettes, etc. From their worry, the consumers would demand change.

Thus, they talked openly about the outbreaks of tuberculosis, which was called the "Tailor's Disease." They told of a young tuberculosis patient making her living through rolling cigarettes. She rolled them with her weak fingers and then used her tongue to wet the paper.

"Would you want to smoke such cigarettes? How can you be sure you haven't already done so?" Smoking at this time was not realized as a health hazard. So the "public relations campaign" was about the danger of disease spreading from the one making the cigarette to the one smoking it. They told about discovering a family producing pricey garments for women in a room where children were very sick from scarlet fever. The sickbed itself doubled as a table for sewing.

Their tactics were effective. It cajoled public sentiment to their cause. Nobody wanted to risk contracting tuberculosis or other diseases from the clothes they bought and wore. In 1902, the Child Labor Committee of the Neighborhood Workers' Association was started. Lillian joined in 1903 as did the famous Jane Addams, her friend from Chicago's Hull House.

But Lillian grew tired of the committee's slow progress. It had no real enforcement power. Though it could cite statistics or make recommendations, they were often ignored. Importantly, there were no nationwide statistics on child labor to back up their claims.

One morning, a random newspaper item caught some of the nurses' attention. It brought to light how the government could be so quick to investigate an agricultural menace yet turn a blind eye to the poverty and suffering that pervaded many neighborhoods. Cotton crops in the

Workers rolling cigars, which often involved young children as laborers, 1889.
(Courtesy of the Jacob Riis Collection at the Museum of the City of New
York and the Visiting Nurse Service of New York Records, Archives & Special
Collections, Health Sciences Library, Columbia University.)

South were being hindered by a kind of insect. The federal government
was looking into the causes and solutions. The US Department of
Agriculture was dispatched for the job.

One of the nurses at the Henry Street Settlement, Florence Kelley,
would sometimes offer biting commentary on the news.

"Civilization is faced with a hideous menace," she reported at the
Settlement over breakfast. "Does anybody want to guess what it is? No,
not poverty. Not disease. Never mind, I'll tell you. The boll weevil."[2]

The boll weevil was an insect hurting crops. The Secretary of
Agriculture announced that he was rushing to Washington to
investigate. The nurses noticed how quickly the government responded.
Whereas when it came to protecting the children, the government was
slow to take action.

The nurses had a moment of realization. They realized a Children's Bureau within the federal government was needed for their cause to be taken seriously. They envisioned a bureau to lobby and pass laws in favor of children. Lillian thought of her close relationship with President Teddy Roosevelt. She recalled that he had always been sympathetic towards young people.

Kelley offered to consult her friend Edward Devine, a renowned sociologist at Columbia University. He admired the Henry Street House and felt their efforts were both well-informed and effective. He liked their idea of setting up a government bureau.

He then called his friend Teddy Roosevelt in the White House. The President was interested, he told Riis, "Bring her down immediately for us to discuss this." Within twenty-four hours, Lillian Wald and the sociologist were in the White House outlining the argument for a national bureau for children. The President agreed, seeing the program's merits. He introduced a bill into Congress.

But even with a US president's support, bills die. This is also true of topics that everyone can support like children's rights. However, powerful interests who benefited from the labor laws did not want to see them changed. They had no problem with the status quo. They blocked any changes.

So despite strong public support, Congress would not open hearings on the bill. Yet, President Roosevelt asked Wald to arrange a Conference on the Care of Dependent Children. Wald and her colleague Florence Kelley traveled to Washington DC in January 1909 to give poignant speeches on behalf of children's rights.

She pleaded, "If money is being spent for the eradication of scabies in cattle, why not spend a small portion of these amounts to save one-fourth of our blind from being blind, to make the deaf hear, and to give to those charged with the care of the wards of the nation, a bureau of central information?"[3]

Changes took time. A year later, she served on a committee of the Second Conference on Charities and Corrections that required children's attendance at school regardless of their income. In other words, poor families could not claim a financial hardship as a reason for keeping their kids out of school. The bill provided aid to families where needed so that their children would attend school. But to reform advocates, it wasn't enough. A Federal Children's Bureau was needed.

Then, in April 1912, it finally happened. President Taft signed into law the bill that Wald and Kelley had advocated for seven years prior. The government was to fund the Federal Children's Bureau. She proclaimed her vision for it as a "great center that would draw from all corners of the earth the latest information on child care, and educate teachers, parents, and health officials on the best methods available. A new conception of the child—free of motion, up-looking, the ward of the nation."[4]

Wald was asked to lead the new organization but turned down the post in order to keep her duties at the Henry Street Settlement. Children were still being exploited in the workplace: in factories, farms, and elsewhere. But now there was a system in place to monitor it.

Indeed, improvements in children's care were numerous. Schools improved, childbirth deaths decreased, and child courts opened. Also, the treatment of orphans and disabled children vastly improved. Finally, legislation was passed controlling the number of hours children could work. The problem was then enforcement of these laws.

Because the Lower East Side economy was fueled by labor intensive garment making, children played a key role in the supply chain. There was much work to be done: cutting, sewing, and finishing for various garments. Much work was done in dark, dirty rooms. Hundreds of children were taught to perform menial tasks before they learned to read. The garment industry was also ultra-competitive. Manufacturers and distributers of garments generally competed on price. This put downward pressure on already very low wages. But families were often caught in this poverty cycle and became dependent on the meager wages. So most kept a blind eye to the working conditions of their children.

Besides garment manufacturing, children were also involved in the selling of newspapers. Often, they had to stand outside in harsh weather conditions to try to sell copies. That business was also hard because "newsies," as they were called, often had to purchase the papers first and then sell them at a mark-up. They would take losses on unsold newspapers. Publishers would at times "squeeze" them by hiking up the wholesale price or the amount they sold the newspapers to the newsies.

Lillian Wald wrote in her book *The House on Henry Street* about the struggle of newsies. "The more they shivered with cold, the greater the harvest of pennies. No wonder that the white-faced little boy stayed out long after his cold had become serious. He himself asked for admission to the hospital, and died there before his absence was noted."[5]

Lillian sought to change the conditions of newsies. Yet, opposition to the regulations and limiting of the sale of papers by little boys on the streets was hard to surmount. Newsboys were glorified in stories. The public did not realize how exploitive the industry was. In reality, many were sleeping on the streets waiting for the next morning's paper to come out.

She was referring to cases like Sammie and his brother who sold newspapers on the street in front of one the largest hotels every night. The cold outside was at times brutal. But they made a key observation. The more they shivered, the more money they would make from the sympathetic. So the boys learned to stay out even when they were sick.

After years, reforms were won. The New York Child Labor Committee passed a law requiring any future newsboy to obtain his parents' and district school superintendents' permission. Many families protested their children selling papers. The boys protested that "others fellows did." Yet, parents were concerned that street work led them into irregular hours and gambling. Other parents disregarded the law and sent their children as newsboys illegally.

The law stated that children had to attend school until they reached the age of fourteen. From ages fourteen to sixteen, they had to obtain working papers. Yet, in reality, many lied about their ages. And parents

As the dust bowl devastated farms, migrant worker camps expanded. Many were in very poor living conditions. The Settlement sent nurses to improve the welfare of these migrant workers. (Courtesy of the Visiting Nurse Service of New York Records, Archives & Special Collections, Health Sciences Library, Columbia University.)

often went along. General society was unsympathetic to this plight. Many believed that the government should not dictate at what age someone would be allowed to start working. If one wanted to work at a younger age, then he or she should be allowed. But this belief system was based on a blind faith that wages were fair and that conditions were humane. It also did not account for families pressuring a child to work who may not want to.

Children were often pressured by their family members to leave school and work. One advancement was the law that no one could work under the age of fourteen and had to produce working papers. The child had to prove by birth certificate that she was the age he or she claimed. Further, the child had to pass a simple test in English and arithmetic and present proof of at least 130 days' school attendance. They also had to be declared physically fit for work by a medical officer. These laws were meant to discourage parents from so easily offering up their children to work for their meager wages.

Yet, many tried to surpass the system. For example, one child, Tommy, appeared at the office for his certification to work. As he got on the scale to be weighed, something did not look right. Given Tommy's slight build, how could the scale weigh so much?

The medical official glanced at his pockets and noticed something bulging.

Tommy looked down. He remained silent.

The official asked what was wrong,

Tommy took out a piece of lead from his pocket.

"Why?" inquired the official looking puzzled

"My mother told me I would probably not weigh enough to pass the doctor."[6]

It turned out that the real reason his mother was going to pull Tommy out of school was that he needed a new pair of shoes.

To combat child labor exploitation, the Henry Street Settlement established scholarships for children from fourteen to sixteen to give training during what they called "two wasted years." Applications were accepted from all parts of Manhattan and the Bronx. Preference was given to children of widows or disabled fathers. Recipients won three dollars per week, which is less than they might be earning. They were supervised throughout the program and encouraged to learn vocational skills. Many were offered vacations in the country.

Lillian tried new tactics to combat this system. She informally divided her opponents as two categories. First, there were the unethical employers. They gamed the system. They typically hid violations from inspectors. They would not allow employees to unionize or even speak of improving their workplace conditions. Lillian sought to expose these actors. The second kind were what she called the "sentimentalists." They believed that poverty was inevitable. Indeed, many believed it was sanctioned by God. Lillian had contempt for both kinds. But she was especially disappointed by the sentimentalists whom she said she should know better.

Lillian reflected on the obstacles to progress for advancing children's rights. She realized there were three chief issues. First, employers saw children as instruments of their profit. They had no incentive to make changes. Second, much of the public believed poverty was a necessary and expected human condition. They did not see a real reason to change it. In fact, many doubted whether change would even be possible. Third, officials charged with enforcing the law were often corrupt and easily paid off.

One day, a child who was making paper bags in a basement with his four siblings rushed to the First Aid Room of the Settlement. A nurse noticed his head was swelled with infections. She asked if the school nurse had noticed his head. When he did not respond, she realized he probably did not go to school. When she asked him if he attended school, he explained why not. "Mother says we gotta work at home. She says she's already getting charity and doesn't want to take more."[7]

The nurses made inquiries into this case. They found out that none of the five children had ever been to school, even though they were all native born. They asked the neighborhood children why no one brought this to their attention. Their answer was that they had not known of this family as the children "never came out to play."

Lillian and her Visiting Nurse Services were focused on providing healthcare to the needy. But the call of social reform would grow louder. Workers were demanding changes.

They could no longer just be nurses.

During this time, Lillian struck a friendship with famed photojournalist and social reformer Jacob Riis. An immigrant from Denmark, Riis arrived in the US in 1870 about two decades before Lillian started her Visiting Nurse Service Henry Street Settlement. It was said that he had only forty dollars and a "locket containing a hair from a woman whom he loved." He worked at several jobs like bricklayer, ironworker, and farmer. These jobs taught him about the struggles of laborers. Within three years, he landed a job as a police reporter. He covered stories of police involvement in the Lower East Side area. He saw a side to the City that few did. He had a keen interest in New York City's tenement life and the rough realities of its residents. It was said that he utilized his camera to inspire profound change. His photos were of everyday residents' struggles often showing them toiling under harsh labor conditions or crammed in a tenement. It was through this visual depiction that the public started to understand the sobering conditions. He "put those conditions on display in a package that was not to be ignored, and his career as a social reformer was launched."[8]

Riis's timing was lucky in that it was during this period that photography was advanced. In Rochester, New York, ironically Lillian Wald's hometown, George Eastman, then a bank clerk, was improving the art. In 1878, Eastman became one of the first to "demonstrate the great convenience of gelatin dry plates over the cumbersome and messy wet plate photography prevalent in his day. Dry plates could be exposed and developed at the photographer's convenience; wet plates had to be coated, exposed at once, and developed while still wet."[9] Several years later, the name "Kodak" was born and along with it easier snapshot photography.

These advances allowed Riis to capture for the public what had been impossible only a short while prior. He started bringing his camera when he traversed the neighborhood streets at night. He pioneered the technology to capture compelling interior and exterior day and night scenes. For night scenes, he was one of the earliest users of flash photography. Prior, the public had only read about these social struggles—if that—now, there was the visual accompaniment. His most famous book was *How the Other Half Lives*, which captured the public's attention on this subject like few books before it. Riis noted that his reason for portraying such a dark tableau was "that every man's experience ought to be worth something to the community from which he drew it, no matter what that experience may be."[10] The book touched not only the public but also politicians. Theodore Roosevelt, then a police commissioner and later the governor of New York State and eventually the president of the United States, famously stated to the photographer, "I have read your book, and I have come to help." The two investigated the stark conditions of the neighborhood, which inspired Roosevelt to act for much of his political career. Riis went on to write other notable books in the same vein including *Children of the Tenements* and *Out of Mulberry Street.*

Riis became a national authority on urban poverty. He lectured regularly on the subject. He also regularly took photographs to rouse public interest in a variety of matters: pollution of the Croton watershed, the source of New York's water supply, or city dumps where health laws were not enforced. He also photographed lodging houses where diseases like typhoid were present.

Other Progressive reformers leveraged photos to advance their causes. Whereas Riis utilized images to supplement his writing and speeches, these reformers put on public exhibitions of photographs as well as architectural models to illuminate slum conditions to a little aware public. As an example, when New York City's Tenement House Department was formed at the turn of the 20th century, the committee hired a photographer to document New York's tenements. Commissioner Robert W. De Forest, a friend of Riis's, observed that "a photograph could convince a negligent landlord to repair his building and worth a dozen lawyers."[11]

Riis partnered with many settlement leaders including Lillian. The two became acquainted shortly after her move to the neighborhood in 1893. They partnered on a variety of issues and both were members of the influential Social Reform Club. Meeting each Tuesday, the club was said by some to be a place where reformers "talked interminably and occasionally dined." Wald, though, stood by the club's mission. She observed that its aims were practical and "looked toward the immediate future with a promise of early success."

Riis and Wald worked not only in community affairs but also in local politics. They aimed to elect reform candidates to municipal office. In 1894, they both supported William Strong, the reform candidate as Mayor of New York City. Once in office, Strong chose Riis's close friend Theodore Roosevelt to serve as Superintendent of New York City's Board of Police. In subsequent years, Riis began to visit the Henry Street Settlement regularly. He brought the budding politician to some of the Settlement's events. Therefore, it was through Riis that the Settlement leaders like Wald would establish to close ties with Roosevelt that would later prove very useful as he advanced to governor and US president.

With her keen networking skills, Wald asked Riis to lobby his friend

Roosevelt when he was Governor of New York to appoint her nurse Florence Kelley as the state's factory inspector. Ultimately, he did not select her. But this networking for political activism continued. Riis continued to be a liaison for Wald when Roosevelt was elected to the highest office in the land as President.

Favors were a two-way street for Riis and Wald. While she asked for political favors from him, he leaned on her for writing key speeches and documentations. In November 1896, Riis asked Wald for her assistance in reporting tenement hallway lighting violations. This was a serious issue in tenements as hallways were often very dark and unsafe. With her day-to-day experience in the neighborhood, she was able to observe and notate. She sent him her speech "Crowded Districts in Large Cities," which Riis read and utilized in his public speaking events. Wald and Riis also testified as witnesses at the New York State Tenement House Commission of 1900. The hearing was "devoted to the subject of the General Evils of the Tenement House System."[12]

The two reformers also partnered on creating inside and outside

Henry Street Settlement district office in a former saloon. During Prohibition, saloons were converted to other uses. (Courtesy of the Visiting Nurse Service of New York Records, Archives & Special Collections, Health Sciences Library, Columbia University.)

spaces for the City's lower class families. Serving as the secretary of the mayor's Advisory Committee on Small Parks, Riis and Wald promoted parks and playgrounds and helped form the Outdoor Recreation League. Funded from private donations, the League bought abandoned urban spaces and turned them into desirable locations for leisure activities like for playgrounds, picnic tables, and more. Their efforts extended to indoor spaces. Skeptical of heavy alcoholic drinking and venues which they felt encouraged it, the two sought to develop spaces as alternatives to saloons for social occasions. They helped raise $100,000, a large sum for 1904, to construct Clinton Hall, which offered "meeting rooms, a dance hall, restaurants, bowling alleys, and billiard rooms."[13]

Their friendship lasted about twelve years from the time Wald moved to the neighborhood until Riis moved to Barre, Massachusetts. He died there in 1914. But Wald and her Settlement carried on his mission. Upon his death, she thanked him "for friendship and encouragement and spirited fellowship for opening up the hearts of a people to emotion, and for the knowledge upon which to guide that emotion into constructive channels."[14]

Chapter 8

Labor Reforms

When Lillian Wald moved into the Lower East Side to serve the community, she was focused on improving their healthcare. Soon after though, she realized that was insufficient. Underlying many of her neighbors' struggles was an exploitive labor system. Both children and adults worked under brutal and often dangerous conditions for very little pay. It became clear that she had to become involved in the labor movement.

When Lillian was living with Mary Brewster on Jefferson Street, they received a visit one evening. Sarah, a neighbor, asked Wald for her assistance in a planned factory strike and in organizing a trade union in their shop.

Sarah discussed the inhumane conditions, the long hours and the dangerous environment. Worse yet was her cruel forewoman. She recounted that a fellow employee tried to speak to the owner but was stopped by the forewoman. Later, the forewoman retaliated by firing her.

She asked for Lillian and Mary to help them "organize in the American way."[1]

Lillian realized her ignorance of trade unions. She asked Mary how they could really help these immigrants without being able to solve their underlying problems like unjust labor laws. She vowed to read up on the subject. She visited the local library the next day and checked out books on trade unions. These books expressed the point of view that in an industrialized society, workers tended to become unimportant as individuals. Individual workers were seen as expendable. Yet, when workers united, they could acquire power and obtain a fairer share of wealth from their labor.

This was interesting yet theoretical. Lillian needed to understand what this meant in everyday terms. So she attended a cigar maker's meeting in the basement. She learned of their struggles and their desire to unify as workers to demand more rights.

Years later, when Lillian was at the Henry Street Settlement, she would revisit these issues. This time, a different young woman named Minnie sought support for her labor unionizing efforts. This time, Lillian was more prepared. They introduced Minnie to a group of philanthropists who were interested in improving worker conditions.

Realizing they would need a safe place to meet, Wald opened up the House's backyard for meetings. She listened to their discussions. She also arranged for leaders in the labor movement to attend meetings to understand these workers' particular concerns.

Wald was walking a fine line. While some of her philanthropists were sympathetic, others were not. They felt their role and those of social organizations was to help the poor fulfill their basic needs when a family's resources were not enough. But they did not want to change the system. Some were concerned about offending influential politicians or about workers starting riots or protests.

Some philanthropists did come to the worker meetings though. Lillian invited Minnie to some of them. At those meetings, Minnie was blunt. "We are in the hands of the boss. What does he care for us? We must work for bread now, but we must think of our future homes. What time has a working girl to make ready for this?"

She continued, "I never had an education. My mother could do nothing but sell potatoes from a pushcart in the street among those rough people." She paused as if she felt guilt. "Of course, some of those people must be nice too, but it is hard to find a diamond in mud."[2]

Several years later, Lillian protested police brutality against girl strikers in the great needle-trades revolt of 1909. She advocated for pushcart safety and protection of the buyers and sellers conducting business on the Lower East Side through the Pushcart Commission. She served on another commission whose mission was to examine the "condition, welfare, and industrial opportunities of aliens in the state of New York."

A key problem was enforcement. These commissions could get legislation passed. Yet, ensuring that people followed the laws was quite a different matter. The use of inspectors to verify adherence to laws was only partially successful. Inspectors became known in neighborhoods. When they were seen in the neighborhood, word was passed along quickly. Work would be taken from children's hands. Other garments would be hidden. Many families working out of their homes were receiving aid from societies. Lillian realized a painful truth. The charitable donations were propping up an exploitive industry.

Deceiving inspectors was not unique to New York's industrial labor. In the South, the problem was also persistent. In the textile mills of the south, child labor was often disguised. One mill owner greeted government inspectors by ordering the flag to be raised under the guise of patriotism. What the inspectors did not know is that the raising of the flag was a signal for the child workers to go home.

Positions Held	Length of Time in Each	Kind of Work
First	3 Days	In factory, sorting buttons
Second	2 Months	Ribboning Corset Covers & Machine Work
Third	1 Week	Ribboning & Buttoning Corset Covers
Fourth	Time Unkown	Ladies Underwear
Fifth	Up to Christmas	Errand Girl
Sixth	2.5 Months	Ribboning Corset Covers
Seventh	Time Unkown	Errand Girl
Eighth	A Few Weeks	Trim, Cut, & Examine Men's Ties
Ninth	A Few Weeks	Return to Second Job
Tenth	A Few Weeks	Ribboning

Typical Employment Record of One Child between Ages 14 and 16[3]

Wald and her organization were caught between two groups. On the one hand, progressives attacked the Settlement house workers for siding with conservative labor to oppose militant union tactics, and for advocating piece-by-piece reform instead of seeking fundamental changes. One trade union organizer criticized the Henry Street Settlement. "It introduces workers to books and flowers and music and gives them a place to leave their babies when they went to work, but it did not raise their wages or shorten their hours." On the other hand, conservatives who supported the Henry Street Settlement called Wald a "radical." Many of her supporters feared labor unions.

Her primary backer, Jacob Schiff, was also reluctant to support the trade union movement. He was concerned that Wald was affiliating herself with unpredictable labor movements. She argued the case for labor movements to him. She pointed out that he wanted to help people help themselves, and that is what they are trying to do in unions.

Her argument was persuasive. Yet, Jacob worried that the strikes would mean revolt and unrest. He also was concerned that his business partners may start scorning him for supporting this organization. He was torn. As a business man and banker, he did not want to see industries disrupted. He wanted to help people. That much was clear. But now he felt in dangerous territory. The very system itself was being questioned. Or possibly overthrown?

Yet, another side of him was sympathetic. He glanced at Lillian and requested that she make lists of the neediest cases among the strikers. He would see that something was done about them—food, money, etc. But he stressed that his name was to be kept anonymous.

She understood his positon. He wanted to help the needy. But he did not want to challenge the system. She had met many who believed that poverty was inevitable. One could apply a Band-Aid but not heal the underlying wound. They believed in charity but not in workers demanding anything. She wrote, "Those who are familiar with factory and shop conditions are convinced that through organization and not through the appeal to pity can permanent reforms be assured."[4]

Lillian realized the need for an accessible public space where people could meet, work out frustrations, and plan. She wrote, "As usual in hard times, it was difficult for the unhappy, dissatisfied unemployed to find a place for the discussion of their troubles."[5] She wanted to provide a meeting place for social functions and labor gatherings. The idea was a forum for public debate that anyone could access. Clinton Hall was erected to serve this purpose. It provided meeting rooms for trade unions, lodges and benefit societies, poolrooms, dining halls, and kitchen preparation.

Then on March 25, 1911 a tragic event would forever change the way the public felt about worker rights and safety. It began as a typical day in the sweatshop in New York's Washington Square neighborhood. Immigrant workers were toiling away making ladies' garments called shirtwaists. That was fashionable ware at the time. The work was arduous, monotonous, and strenuous. It was very low-paying. Worse yet, the owners of the factory, Max Blanck and Isaac Harris, locked their workers in. That was, of course, a fire hazard. They did so, they said, to prevent workers from stealing. An unstated reason was also to keep out union organizers. Workers were often punished or fired for even mentioning the word "union." The owners feared that if workers were to organize, they would gain too much power in demanding changes.

Around 4:45 p.m. just before closing, one of the greatest tragedies was about to unfold. Probably from a cigarette or a hay wired sewing machine, a fire broke out. The flames began to grow. Panicked, the workers ran towards the door to escape. But the door was locked. The owners had escaped through the rooftop. They never unlocked the doors.

The fire started to overtake the floor. The fire trucks arrived. But their ladders could not reach beyond the sixth floor. In the chaos, many jumped out the window. Bystanders and firemen watched helplessly from the streets. Sadly, there were corpses lining the streets. Before it was over, 146 workers perished. Most were Jewish or Italian immigrants, and women from age fifteen to forty-three.

The owners were brought to court to find out if they were at fault. They hired a well-known defense attorney. They argued in court that the owners did not know the door was locked at the time of the fire. Thus, they were not responsible. Several survivors of the fire testified at the trial. Yet, their knowledge of English was very limited. They gave their best account of what happened. But the defense lawyers asked them to rephrase their testimonies. They could not. So the defense team argued that their statements were "rehearsed" and that they were "told what to say."

In the criminal court system in the United States, the defendant is presumed innocent until otherwise proven guilty by a jury of twelve of his or her peers. All twelve jurors must agree that the evidence shows the defendant is guilty beyond a "reasonable doubt." If the jury cannot agree that the evidence shows guilt, the defendant is presumed "not guilty" or is acquitted.

Because of the defense team's legal skills and the prosecutor's inability to show the owners knew the doors were locked, the owners were acquitted. They also were awarded a substantial sum from their fire insurance company. Sadly, two years later, they were rearrested for locking in employees.

Though very tragic, the event did promote more sympathy for workers' rights. Ironically, before this accident occurred, the women in the factory had tried to organize a union to protest against dangerous shop conditions. They were unable to do so.

After the tragedy, the public was more sympathetic. So was the government. The federal, state, and local governments stepped up safety standards and enforcements. Union leaders demanded more changes. Organizations like the International Ladies' Garment Workers Union won more concessions for their members in ensuing years.

Wald recalls these events in her book *The House on Henry Street*. A meeting was called at the Metropolitan Opera House by those "horrified men and women of the city." At the meeting, a "young cap maker stood at the edge of the great opera house stage and in a voice hardly raised, though it reached every person in that vast audience, arraigned society for regarding human life so cheaply."[6] As a result, worker conditions started to improve. Plus, serious discussions over minimum wages began.

This activism led Lillian to play a larger role in the women's suffrage movement. She realized that if women could not vote, their opinions would not be taken seriously by public officials. Nor would they be able to force meaningful change in the system.

Other nurses at the Settlement like Lavinia spearheaded this issue. Lavinia's participation in labor movement strikes, protests, and parades sometimes clashed with the law. One day, a neighborhood police captain came to the Settlement house. He looked uncomfortable and said he did not want to have to arrest Lavinia.

Lillian knew her housemate at the Settlement and friend, Lavinia Dock, was in trouble for marching in a demonstration for women's right to vote. She was okay with being arrested if that's what it took. In fact, she may have wanted to get arrested in order to bring more publicity to her cause. Lillian smiled. She was proud of Lavinia.

While the fight for labor and women's rights continued, another battle was brewing. Reformers wanted to prohibit the sale and manufacture of alcoholic beverages. The movement was borne out of what they saw. Many families went hungry because the father had spent the little money he had earned on drinking. They witnessed many reckless brawls on the street.

In her autobiography *Windows on Henry Street*, Lillian recounts the Curry family's struggle with alcohol. They led a carefree life until the husband started drinking. She notes that he was a "generous and well-meaning man toward his family but treats and invitations from his friends in the saloon were irresistible."[7] His wages were squandered at the saloon. She contrasts this life with life after the Prohibition amendment was passed. "The whole family life is changed—the day-to-day experience and the outlook for the children." She notes that he

Esteemed nurse Lavinia Dock at the Settlement during her later years. (Courtesy of the Visiting Nurse Service of New York Records, Archives & Special Collections, Health Sciences Library, Columbia University)

Prohibition was a "constitutional ban on the production, importation, transportation, and sale of alcoholic beverages" from 1920 to 1933. Private ownership and consumption of alcohol was still allowed. This encouraged individuals and clubs to stock up before the ban was in place. It was passed by an unlikely alliance of rural Protestants and social progressives. Though its purpose was to improve rampant alcoholism, it was widely ignored and gave rise to organized crime which illegally kept the liquor flowing.

was so happy that he bought a radio for his family to enjoy music from, a luxury at the time for that neighborhood.

She emphasized these sentiments in an article called "I Speak for Four Million." She painted the pre-prohibition scene. "On Saturday nights the saloons' power was most obvious. The trucks gathered around the curb while the men went inside with their pay envelopes. That night scene has disappeared since the passage of the amendment and with it the Sunday brawls, the tragic Monday mornings when in factory or workshop women appeared for an advance on their husbands' pay because he had spent all his pay in the saloon."[8]

Lillian rejoiced at the passing of the Prohibition Amendment in 1919 and balked at its repeal in 1933. But Lillian and her fellow nurses were fighting a losing battle. Most of the public was against the amendment believing that the government over-reached. It also did not stop the consumption of alcohol. People simply imbibed alcoholic products in secret often in speakeasies. This gave rise to illegal markets controlled by the mob and other forces. Ultimately, the anti-prohibitionists won out.

Chapter 9

The Rise of World War I

As 1916 approached, Lillian Wald would find controversy over her opposition to World War I. It would rattle her causes and much that she had worked for. It also altered her relationships with the philanthropists who had helped her mission. She did not want to jeopardize her organization, yet she could not stand by the war on principle. How did the war start and how did the United States become involved?

It started as a regional skirmish among European nations. On June 28, 1914, Archduke Franz Ferdinand of Austria and his wife Sophie, heirs to the throne of Austria-Hungary, were assassinated in Sarajevo, Yugoslavia by Gavrilo Princip, a Yugoslav nationalist. For a decade, tensions were brewing among the Great Powers of Italy, France, Germany, Britain, Austria-Hungary, and Russia over European and colonial issues. Though the conflict started with Austria-Hungary, Serbia, and Russia competing for land and regional influence, the other Great Powers were pulled into the conflict through various treaties and obligations they had signed.

At first, most thought the conflict would last only months and be confined to Europe. They were wrong on both accounts. The Great War, as it was called, began to encompass countries globally. The Allies fought the Central Powers often in trenches. The war was brutal. What became known as the "Western Front" between Germany and France would see gruesome fighting for three years. It was one of the deadliest conflicts in history with more than nine million combatants and seven million civilians dead from the war.

The war tactics were different from those of previous conflicts. Weapons of mass destruction were used for the first time. Firebombs, chemical weapons, and mustard gas were among the most lethal. Moreover, airstrikes against civilian populations meant to destroy morale were deployed.

Against the backdrop of this war, the United States wanted to remain neutral. President Woodrow Wilson sought to broker a peace

The First World War or the "Great War" ravaged Europe from July 1914 until November 1918 in one of the largest wars in history. It was also the most technologically advanced wars in history and is marked by the use of chemical weapons and arduous trench warfare. The US involvement spawned what is considered one of the greatest propaganda war efforts to enlist recruitment.

deal. Yet, both sides of the War remained obstinate. The stakes were raised when German U-boats sank the British liner *Lusitania* in 1915 with 128 Americans aboard. Wilson refrained from war. He used the phrase, "America is too proud to fight." Most Americans, like Lillian, believed the US should stay out of the war.

But in early 1917, that opinion changed, spurred by the German attacks in Belgium and the German submarine sinking of the *Lusitania*, a British ocean liner. Former president Theodore Roosevelt, who knew Wald well and was sympathetic to many of her causes, was a major voice for entering the war.

The United States' fate was sealed. It could no longer avoid entering the war. President Wilson delivered the message. "With a profound sense of the solemn and even tragic character of the step I am taking and of the grave responsibilities which it involves that the United States will employ all its resources to bring the government of the German Empire to terms and end the war."[1]

Only six out of one hundred senators and fifty representatives opposed the war. On April 6, 1917, as the president declared war, Lillian Wald and her colleagues remained against the war. This created a whole new challenge for the Henry Street Settlement and for the philanthropists who supported them.

Lillian and her colleagues found themselves on the sidelines as the declaration of war created a new reality for the nation. President Woodrow Wilson told the editor of the *New York World*, "Once lead this people into war, and they'll forget there ever was such a thing as tolerance. To fight you must be brutal and ruthless, and the spirit of ruthless brutality will enter into the very fiber of our national life, infecting Congress, the courts, the policeman, and the man on the streets."[2]

Initially, public opinion was mixed on the merits of the war. As soldiers were deployed to Europe, most went along with it. The Lower East Side began to change as the drama of the war pervaded the nation.

Despite the sweeping patriotism tide, Lillian held to her belief that the war would not accomplish anything in the long run. She called war "a disease from which man must be cured." People lashed out her. They called her "unpatriotic" and a host of other unflattering terms.

Peace activists like Lillian and Jane Addams were deeply concerned that entering the war would distract the national attention from social and labor issues in favor of military concerns. They also predicted it would drain government resources leaving little left over for social needs. They reflected on how each saw different people living together harmoniously in their respective neighborhoods: in New York for Lillian Wald and in Chicago for Jane Addams. They reasoned, "If individuals could enjoy good relations, nations could as well." Wald drew a link between the neighborhoods she served and internationalism. "People who lived in Settlements were internationalist in outlook because they knew that the fundamental problems of all peoples were the same."

Notably, not all nurses at the Henry Street Settlement opposed the war. Some changed their minds once the US entered it. Lavinia Dock, for example, opposed US military interventionism at first but then called for a "fight until the finish."

But Lillian was sympathetic to injured soldiers. She did not want to see them suffer. She also had mixed emotions about sending many doctors and nurses into the war. First, that would risk their lives. Second, it would prolong the war. Serving on the Red Cross Advisory Committee, she protested the move to send nurses to Europe through the Red Cross. Still, twenty percent of the nation's nurses were in the military at this time.

She, as did many, objected to that fact that women could not vote. They would have to bear the suffering of war through losing husbands, children, and other loved ones. Further, some would play an active role on the battlefield through nursing and other functions. Even for those back home, life would involve wartime necessary sacrifices like rations on food. Yet, women could have no voice in the decision.

She led a peace march down Fifth Avenue hoping to influence policymakers. She also formed a coalition called the Women's Peace Party. Prominent women social reformers took part. Jane Addams was elected national chairman. The *Washington Post* reported that meeting as an effort to "enlist all American women to arouse the nation to respect the sacredness of human life and to abolish war."[3] The group demanded a say in deciding key matters of policy. The group proclaimed "We demand that women be given a share in deciding between war and peace in all the courts of high debate—within the home, the school, the church, the industrial order, and the state."

But opposing the war had a price. The Military Intelligence Service drew up a list of sixty-two persons accused of having been "active in movements which did not help the US when the country was fighting." Lillian's name was on this list. In fact, some considered Lillian and others who opposed the war dangerous. A *New Yorker* article noted: "When the name of Lillian Wald was found inscribed on the blacklist of dangerous characters, jeers and catcalls went up from the public."[4] The article asked how someone who was looked up to by bankers, social leaders, and politicians as well as "nice old ladies," could now be seen as dangerous. Much of it was war-infused hysteria.

Lillian and Jane Addams remained staunchly against the war despite growing criticism against them and their organizations. Their philanthropists grew increasingly worried about associating themselves with marginalized "nay-sayers" of the impending war. Yet Lillian was not dissuaded. She actually took pride in being on a list with others whom she respected like Jane Addams. She believed that ultimately the public would "come around" in their thinking. But most of those who always supported Lillian and her efforts stood by her.

At a publicized meeting, Jane Addams called for a "council of neutral nations" to discuss how to avert war. She quoted leaders from other countries. "This was an old man's war that the young men who were dying were not the men who wanted war, and were not the men who believed in war." The press was attacking peace activists like Lillian and her cohorts. The *New Jersey Herald* called them "serious enemies of the Republic, honest as they may be in their opinions."

Yet, Lillian countered in articles. She warned in an article called "Seeing Red" that "when militarism comes in at the door, democracy flies out of the window." She noted that welfare programs were being discarded in favor of militaristic expenditures. "A wave of hysteria is sweeping over the country under the seemingly reasonable name of preparedness. When you put a gun into a man's hand you give him the best argument for shooting."[5]

When she and Florence Kelley testified before the House and Senate Military Affairs Committee, the *Post* described them in more flattering terms. "It would be hard to find two women who are more devoted patriots and are working longer hours for the advancement of America every day in the year."

As the months drew on, public support increased towards the war effort. Industry, banking, and other forces formed a powerful pro-war lobby. The United States government hired them to prepare for the war. This increase in employment gained the support of labor unions.

Importantly, Lillian did not try to stop individuals who wanted to enlist. A young man told her, "I know how you feel about armies; but I do not feel that way. I want to enlist. Do you mind?"

"Of course not! Follow your convictions. Nothing should hold you back from doing what you think is right," she responded.[6]

President Woodrow Wilson was reluctant to meet with Wald and her compatriots due to his fear of a backlash. Paradoxically, he had campaigned on peace. Slogans like "He Kept Us out of War" and "Internationalism Abroad and Progressivism at Home" were popular. A political advertisement offered "a choice between Hughes, Roosevelt, and war or Wilson and peace with honor." Wald, though, remained a supporter of Wilson. She saw him as the best chance to avoid an unnecessary escalation of war.

To convince the public of the necessity of war, a massive propaganda campaign was launched. George Creel, a journalist with liberal connections, was tapped to lead a Committee on Public Information. He recruited across fields from journalists, educators, artists, and public relations experts. Some were "muckrakers." That was a term from this period for American journalists who tried to expose social wrong-doings, scandals, and corruption. War propaganda tactics utilized included posters, bulletins, and local speakers. Then, the Sedition Act of May 1918 made dissension from the war more dangerous. It became almost illegal to criticize the government.

Private citizens joined in what became a mini-witch hunt. Individuals spied on each other and reported on any "radical dissenters." Many were fired from their posts for their spoken beliefs about the war. The right to free speech, though guaranteed by the constitution, seemed to be ignored in the name of national security.

Lillian was caught in a double bind. She wanted to speak out against the war she did not believe in. Yet, she didn't want to put her organization in jeopardy. After careful consideration along with twenty colleagues, she wrote President Wilson noting how rights have been taken away. They recounted that "halls have been refused for public discussion, meetings have been broken up, speakers arrested, and censorship exercised to prevent free discussion."

The President agreed to act. Soon after though, conscription was passed. This meant males of a certain age were drafted into the army.

The Settlement seemed caught in the middle. Many of the immigrants whom they served wanted to enlist. For them, it was a patriotic act for their new country. Lillian obliged. She converted one of the Settlement's houses to the draft board and conducted hurried weddings and farewell parties. She wrote that she was "depressed and overwhelmed" by the taking away of her civil liberties.

Her letter in the early days of the war shows her reluctance to commit nurses to the effort. "War is war! We who hate it, who would make every sacrifice in order to prevent it and make future wars absolutely impossible, must guard every act that we do, every impulse that moves us to discover whether directly or indirectly we are supporting war. I think we must acknowledge that when we send relief surgeons and nurses, the best that we have, to the fields of battle, we are glorifying war and its barbarisms."[7]

Wald and her Settlement were far from the only war skeptics. Young males who objected to war on religious or moral grounds were "conscientious objectors." Generally, the government did not view this as a valid reason for skipping military service. Lillian spoke out for this group that the US "should not coerce men's conscience in a war for freedom." Roger Baldwin was a "conscientious objector." He was sentenced to one year in prison. Lillian visited him.

Against the backdrop of war, the Visiting Nurse Service was becoming increasingly famous. It expanded efforts throughout New York City. It also helped change the mission of key organizations like the Red Cross. Until this time, the Red Cross was chiefly involved in wartime activities. Lillian persuaded the organization to participate in public health issues as well. Soon after, the Red Cross was involved in teaching hygiene and caring for the sick.

In 1910, the Department of Nursing and Health was created at Teachers College, Columbia University providing professional training and requirements. Nursing was gaining traction as an important field. Capitalizing on this momentum, Wald saw the Red Cross as a way to advance nursing as a profession. She espoused the importance of advertising to promote the value of nursing. She looked to the Red Cross marketing as an example.

"Would it not be advisable for the Red Cross to have a great deal of publicity upon the training of nurses for public health work? Their last pamphlet is excellent but I should say that the nursing world, training

As part of advertising efforts, Henry Street Settlement held a poster contest for the best logo. (Courtesy of the Visiting Nurse Service of New York Records, Archives & Special Collections, Health Sciences Library, Columbia University)

schools, and so forth ought to get the benefit of the Red Cross publicity experts. The main facts would be to advertise."

As the war dragged on, Lillian and her colleagues started the "Save the Baby Campaign." Every child under the age of five in New York City was to be examined. As a result, thousands of babies were medically examined and their parents received home care instructions when needed. Through the campaign, health care workers were educated on infant health. This played an especially important role during wartime when families were divided as fathers were at war and mothers were drawn into the workplace.

Despite these gains, Lillian was in conflict. Her leadership at the peace advocacy group, the American Union Against Militarism (AUAM) was increasingly at odds with her leadership at the Settlement. AUAM was becoming more anti-government by the month. Lillian was worried that this could hurt the Settlement. She had to decide.

A long-time supporter of the Settlement, J. Horace withdrew his support of the Settlement. A noted banker and chairman of the board of the American Railway Express, he wrote that Miss Wald and the AUAM were "disloyal and bordering on treason."

Lillian tried to change his mind. She explained that she was trying to preserve liberties and freedom of speech. She could not change his mind. Worse yet, her long-time supporter Jacob Schiff had increasing doubts. He told her, "No one can foretell what may be yet before us and what everyone may be called upon to do for our Country."[8] To not antagonize her supporters and for differences in opinion, Lillian resigned from AUAM.

By this point, the Henry Street Settlement was changing. Many of her closest friends had left. Lavinia Dock, her closest friend, moved to her family homestead in Pennsylvania. She wrote a note to Lillian explaining that she was still committed to the movement but had retired from nursing. The two remained friends.

Chapter 10

Postwar Life at the Settlement

By mid-1918, the war was winding down. After years of a brutal war with very heavy losses and injuries on both sides, an armistice was signed on November 11, 1918. Though the war was over, the government's suspicion of dissent was not. There was a "Red Scare." This means the government was concerned about communists or Russian revolutionaries infiltrating the ranks of US government and other institutions. It was a climate of fear in which dissent continued to not be tolerated.

Lillian's name was tarnished by a list produced by New York State of suspicious people. A committee was formed to identify "radicalism" in Settlement houses and schools. An article in June 1921 in the *New York Evening Telegram* labeled her and Jane Addams "anxious to bring about the overthrow of the government and establish in this country a Soviet government on the same lines in Russia."

She wrote to a friend, "My political attitude is making some of our generous friends uneasy and one of our largest givers—nearly $15,000 a year—has withdrawn because I am 'socially inclined.' Poor things, I am sorry for them. It is foolish since, after all, counting things in the large and wide, I am at least one insurance against unreasonable revolution in New York."

In 1920, another victory for the Progressive movement was won. State legislatures and Congress ratified the 19th amendment to the Constitution giving all women across the nation the right to vote. Prior, only select states provided voting rights to women. Requiring thirty-six of the fifty state legislatures to approve the measure once passed by Congress, Tennessee became the 36th state to do so on August 18, 1920. It was on that day that ratification was completed.

This legislative victory was well-received at the Henry Street Settlement. But bad news was to follow. Sadly, in September 1920, Jacob Schiff died after persistent sleeplessness and pain. She mourned his death. On a practical note, her chief supporter from the beginning was now gone. Other philanthropists were uneasy. But Mr. Schiff's estate had bequeathed a gift of $300,000 to the Henry Street Settlement for the construction of a central administration building for the Visiting Nurse Service.

As the 1920s drew on, the period of Progressivism began in the mid-1890s with its emphasis on helping the disenfranchised drew to a close. The economy was starting to boom. Buildings were erected at a startling speed. Builders of skyscrapers outdid each other for the tallest structure. The presidents, Warren Harding, Calvin Coolidge, and Herbert Hoover, ushered in postwar conservatism. The public was interested in acquiring wealth, spending, and speculative investing. Popular sayings were "two cars in every garage" and a "chicken in every pot." The decade became known as the "Roaring Twenties."

Amidst these changes, Lillian and the Henry Street continued its work. But it was not the same. Lost in the intoxication of the Roaring Twenties was interest in helping the disadvantaged. The Lower East Side that Lillian worked in for decades was also changing. Many of the immigrant families had moved out to places with more space uptown or the outlying boroughs of New York. Immigration dramatically slowed with the Immigration Act of 1924 putting quotas on the number allowed to enter the United States each year.

The social work that Lillian knew was also changing. It became less about social reform and more about solving an individual's problems. But the Henry Street Settlement was expanding. 265 Henry Street was converted into residence quarters for the staff, a gymnasium, meeting rooms, and a kindergarten. The building next door was converted into a center for workers' education and the instruction of arts and crafts.

The neighborhood also began to change its appearance. Though tenements remained, they were cleaner and plumbing was common. Due to changes pushed through by ardent housing advocates, toilets were installed inside of apartment buildings. Trucks were prohibited from parking in the neighborhood thereby relieving congestion.

The neighborhood was a stepping stone for many immigrants. Families hoped to move to places with more space. Some moved to Brooklyn particularly when the Williamsburg Bridge opened in 1901. In the mid-1920s, due to changes in the law, immigration slowed considerably. English became a more common language to hear in the neighborhood. It became more homogenous.

Just as the neighborhood changed so did the status of nursing.

Garment vendors in the Lower East side in 1938. By this time, many of the huge crowds of shoppers and peddlers were gone. New immigrants slowed to a halt. (Courtesy of the Visiting Nurse Service of New York Records, Archives & Special Collections, Health Sciences Library, Columbia University.)

Lillian had created a "profession" for nursing. She noted at Teachers College at Columbia University: "The nurse is a woman of rounded and self-balanced personality, creative, initiating ideas, able to lead, develop and direct her nursing service toward a goal of social betterment. No longer is nursing a mere hand-maiden but a trusted and indispensable ally to medical science." Education for nurses also improved markedly. Hospitals offered better facilities and lengthened their training courses. The first nursing school to demand college education of its applications was the School of Nursing at Yale.[1]

A telegram in 1913 from Lillian to a senator portrays her passion for improving the educational standards for nursing. Just as other fields had exams and minimum requirements, she argued that nursing needed similar measures. "We believe that the community demands thoroughly trained nurses and that the Regents (New York State examiners) should be held responsible for the character and quality of the training schools as they are for other educational institutions." She further notes that the public must be protected from the "quack nurse."[2]

Public health nursing improved too. These nurses studied not just patients' illnesses but the communities in which they lived. They were "guardians of the community." Public health was offered for the first time at universities.

In 1923, she suffered a deep family loss with her mother dying. She wrote, "The world seemed to change and though other affections remained, there was none like her. She was very dear and had a genius for loving and sympathy that was extraordinary. The world seems poorer for having so much love and sweetness removed from it."[3] A year later, her younger brother, Gus, died. Her sister Julia was Lillian's only remaining family member.

There were significant changes in Lillian's personal life too. Starting in the mid-1920s while in her sixties, Lillian's health began to falter. She was quite ill in 1925 after a serious operation, but she recovered.

She gradually spent less time at Henry Street and more time at her vacation home in the House-on-the-Pond in Westport, Connecticut. It was her favorite place. Westport children were always welcome to swim during the summer and skate on the pond's ice during the winter.

Yet, parts of the Henry Street Settlement were thriving. The Neighborhood Playhouse that she had helped start boasted some of the finest performances. The clubs at the Settlement were also flourishing. About 1,500 young people were enrolled in the Settlement's clubs in 1926.

Then, at the closing of the 1920s, the world changed instantly. On October 24, 1929, the stock market crashed which ushered in the Great Depression, the worst economic times the nation had ever seen. Many lost their entire savings. Breadlines and make-shift tents for those who lost their homes became commonplace.

The neighborhood suffered greatly during the Great Depression of the 1930s. Suddenly, the case loads of Visiting Nurse Service workers at the Henry Street Settlement skyrocketed. Compounding the problem were other social services agencies who cratered under financial woes and referred clients to the Henry Street Settlement. Fundraising was also drying up. Suddenly, many former donors announced they needed to curtail or cease their giving due to the extreme financial conditions. Wald was filled with despair.

She wrote, "I don't know what we'll do unless we get more money, the situation is tragic. We have bare one-third of our money, and we will have to keep on asking people who gave small sums to give larger ones. It's the worst winter (1932) I have had and, as you know, we began during a terrible time in 1893."[4]

After years of rapid growth, the Great Depression in the US started with the stock market crash in October 1929. It was largely brought on by rampant speculation and over leveraging whereby consumers and businesses took on too much debt. People suffered through high unemployment, poverty, and a general despair for several years.

Yet, she recounts acts of generosity even among those that had little to give. One evening there was a knock on the door of the Henry Street House. Florence Kelley answered. A "tired and shabby stranger" stood before her.

"Is this the house that's good to all nations?" he asked.

"Yes, I think it is," said Mrs. Kelley.

"Well," said the man, "I've brought it a dollar."[5]

She invited him in, but he declined. He had walked weary miles from another part of the city. He did not want his name known. No one ever saw him again.

A woman wrote to the Settlement:

"I see in the papers that you need money. You took care of my little boy when he was so bad (sic) burned and all my life since then I pray God, make me rich so I can help you big. But he hasn't answered my prayer so I send this which I know isn't much but it is all I have."[6] Enclosed in the letter was a ten dollar bill.

Lillian wrote in her 1934 autobiography *Windows on Henry Street*, "It is hard to know whether to laugh or weep over those who, poor in money but rich in good will, have given what they held most dear."[7]

Many changes were afoot at the Settlement as it persevered through very tough economic times. Lillian ceased officially to be the head worker at the Henry Street Settlement. She presented it as a happy occasion. "I have had love and fellowship beyond my deserts," she would say. She chose Helen Hall of Philadelphia as her successor. She wrote her friend Jane Addams a letter explaining her decision.

"I know you'll be glad because she is a fine person and an enthusiast about the contribution of Settlements. Perhaps you have been reading her articles about the dole and the bread lines. I think they are very good. We have organized in this fashion; that she is to be Head Worker and I remain President of the Settlement."

By 1931, there were nearly 10,000 public nurses in the US, and the numbers increased steadily thereafter. This was about seven times the number just twenty years prior when there were 1,413 public nurses registered in the country.

Governor of New York Al Smith and Lillian Wald at the Visiting Nurse Service building in its new offices at 99 Park Ave, during the late 1920s. The organization operated "health clinics, baby welfare stations, first aid rooms, polio clinics, after-care influenza clinics, intensive maternity work, and a developing industrial service." (Courtesy of the Visiting Nurse Service of New York Records, Archives & Special Collections, Health Sciences Library, Columbia University.)

Beyond the numbers, Lillian improved the status of nurses. Not long before, the profession was regarded as not much more than menial work. It was not considered worthy of rigorous training. It had little to no voice in health policies.

In the mid-1930s, she wrote a sequel to her first book *The House on Henry Street*. Her new book *Windows on Henry Street* was based on the notion that the "windows of Henry Street look out at the whole world."

But this time, Lillian did not have the vigor she once did. She spent more time in her Connecticut home. She loved to appreciate nature especially the flowers. Yet, the comforts of her country home could not shield her from the realities of the Settlement back in New York City.

Henry Street Settlement on NBC Radio in 1933. The agency used all forms of the advertising channels including the radio to recruit nurses and to raise awareness about its services. (Courtesy of the Visiting Nurse Service of New York Records, Archives & Special Collections, Health Sciences Library, Columbia University.)

The Henry Street Settlement was sorely lacking funds. The city and state turned down funding requests.

In 1937, she celebrated her seventieth birthday at the Henry Street Settlement and throughout all its branches. She received birthday messages from around the world. Many of her contemporaries had died by that point including Jane Addams and Florence Kelley.

She also had another gift on her seventieth birthday from none other than President Franklin Roosevelt. She tuned into his special radio broadcast. The President's mother read a message to her and the whole world. It was an acclaim to her. Governor Herbert Lehman of New York and Mayor Fiorello La Guardia of New York also presented her with the distinguished service certificate of the City of New York.

She was pleased that society had changed from the early days of her work in the Lower East Side. Under President Franklin Roosevelt's New Deal, new social programs were introduced. Unemployment insurance, bank deposit insurance, agricultural insurance, social security, and other programs firmed up the social nets.

President Franklin D. Roosevelt composed a letter to Lillian in 1937 thanking her for her public service efforts. He signed it "her old friend, Franklin D. Roosevelt." (Courtesy of the Visiting Nurse Service of New York Records, Archives & Special Collections, Health Sciences Library, Columbia University.)

Yet, she was alarmed by the growing anti-Semitism in Europe under the rise of the Nazi party. In Germany, the government was turning against Jewish citizens and stripping away many of their rights. She spoke out against the trouble brewing in Germany. She wrote to Governor Lehman, "Such a hectic time as we are having. I feel it in bed as much as you would feel it where the winds do blow."[8] Yet, she may never have learned about the outbreak of World War II. Aware of her impassioned peace stance, her friends concerned about her health may have kept newspapers and current affairs from her.

In September 1940, Lillian Wald died of a cerebral hemorrhage. Thousands mourned her passing. Rabbi Stephen Wise of the Free Synagogue held a service for her. At a Carnegie Hall Memorial meeting, 2,500 people assembled to honor her legacy. Mayor La Guardia held the services. She was called "one of the great women of all time, and they told of her leadership in struggles that know no end."[9]

President Franklin D. Roosevelt noted, "Lillian Wald became one of the outstanding social workers of the country because she had a heart overflowing with compassion. The Henry Street Settlement has a superb record in bringing light to dark places and joy to hearts that had only known sorrow. As one who was privileged to call her a friend, I consider it also a privilege to join with those honoring her memory."[10]

In the decades since, her legacy has endured. In the neighborhood she ardently served, a new playground was opened in "appreciation of her pioneer work for children and district nursing in this city." Public housing opened in the same neighborhood. Though its long-term benefits have been controversial, they were a vast improvement to the squalid tenements that preceded them. School nurses, subsidized or free lunches, and special education classes are a staple of schools across the nation. Workers enjoyed more rights and protections.

Today, the Henry Street Settlement that she once moved into with Mary Brewster still stands. It performs social services and community functions for all ethnicities and ages. More than a century later, the performing arts center is thriving putting on critically acclaimed performances. Like its origins, it is a performance space where a famed actor can work side by side with a neighborhood resident. Like Wald once envisioned, the Settlement is a place where neighbors can find solace. The Visiting Nurse Service spun off from the Henry Street Settlement in 1944. Today, there are Visiting Nurse Service agencies globally providing home health care and therapies to patients wherever

New York State Governor Herbert Lehman gives a speech on WNYC radio in 1940 about Wald and the significance of the Henry Street Settlement Visiting Nurse Service to the public. (Courtesy of the Visiting Nurse Service of New York Records, Archives & Special Collections, Health Sciences Library, Columbia University.)

they call home. In New York City alone, the organization services more than 35,000 patients on any given day. In 1970, thirty years after her death, Wald was elected to the Hall of Fame for Great Americans.

A professor of Public Health at the Yale School of Medicine wrote "The House on Henry Street has become one of the great world centers of nursing education. Over 2,000 graduate nurses have had experience at Henry Street as members of the staff. The supervisors who have received training have gone out to fill some of the most important educational positions in the nursing field. In every place where a nurse brings beneficent aid in the crisis of childbirth, her delicate techniques are influenced by the Settlement. The whole brilliant evolution of public health nursing bears the impress of leadership from the House on Henry Street."[11]

Perhaps her most significant legacy is something deeper than statistics or awards bestowed. She saw the promise of humanity when few did not. She envisioned a nursing service that would care for the whole individual not just his or her physical ailments. She saw the need to nurture their creativity and artistic talents. She also promoted a vision of racial integration, equality for women, and rights for children.

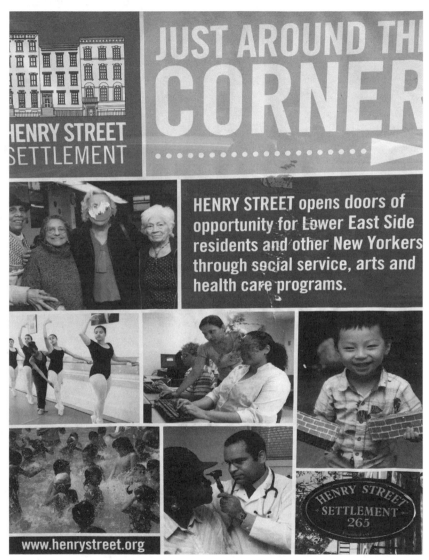

Today, Henry Street Settlement serves a variety of people throughout New York City in arts, healthcare, and social service programs. (Photo by Paul Kaplan.)

Though obvious today, they were little discussed and sometimes controversial positions during her time.

Her name is not well known among the public today. But her deeds are. Perhaps, that is the way Lillian would have wanted it.

Notes

Chapter 1

1. Beryl Williams, *Lillian Wald: Angel of Henry Street* (New York: Julian Messner, 1948), 30.

Chapter 2

1. Ibid., 5.
2. Beatrice Siegel, *Lillian Wald of Henry Street* (New York: Macmillan Publishing, 1983), 16.
3. Ibid., 18.
4. Ibid., 50.
5. Williams, 63.
6. Ibid., 66.

Chapter 3

1. Siegel, 26.
2. Williams, 79.
3. Ibid, 84.
4. Ibid, 88.
5. Lillian Wald: *An Angel of Henry Street*, 98.
6. Ibid, 100.
7. Ibid.
8. Wald letters to Jacob Schiff, Wald papers, Reel 1, Box 1-2, New York Public Library.
9. Letter to Jacob Schiff and Solomon Loeb, New York, November 3, 1893.
10. Ibid.

Chapter 4

1. Lillian Wald, *The House on Henry Street* (New York: Henry Holt and Company, 1915), 15.
2. Ibid.
3. Ibid.
4. Ibid.
5. Ibid.
6. Williams, 18.
7. Lillian Wald, *The House on Henry Street* 22.

Chapter 5

1. Williams, 121.
2. Lillian Wald, *The House on Henry Street* 46.
3. Lavinia Dock, The Nurses Settlement in New York File 1, Drawer 1, Nursing Archives, Special Collections, Teachers College, Columbia University, 4.
4. Jacob Schiff letters to Lillian Wald, Wald papers, Reel 1, Box 1-2, New York Public Library.
5. "Profiles: Rampant but Respectable," *The New Yorker*, December 14, 1929.

6. Doris Daniels, *Always a Sister: The Feminism of Lillian D. Wald* (New York: Feminist Press at the City University, 1989).

7. Metropolitan Life Insurance website, www.metlife.com/about/corporate-profile/metlife-history/helping-healing-people.

8. Ibid.,

9. *The House on Henry Street*, 63.

10. Ibid., 16.

Chapter 6

1. Ibid., 80.

2. Ibid.

3. www.henrystreet.org/about/our-buildings/301-henry-street.

4. Williams, 166.

5. Letter to Edgerton Winthrop Jr., February 15, 1905, New York Public Library Archives.

6. Ibid.

7. Lillian Wald, *Windows on Henry Street* (Boston: Little, Brown & Co., 1933), 172.

8. Lillian Wald, *House on Henry Street*, 187.

9. Ibid., 103.

Chapter 7

1. Wald letters to Jacob Schiff, Wald papers, Reel 1, Box 1-2, New York Public Library Archives.

2. Lillian Wald: *Angel of Henry Street*, 172.

3. *The House on Henry Street*, 172.

4. Ibid.

5. *The House on Henry Street*, 148.

6. Ibid., 136.

7. Ibid., 178.

8. Tony Moore, Jacob Riis Biography website, A&E Television Networks, November 2015.

9. Eastman Kodak website, www.kodak.com/corp/aboutus/heritage.

10. Tony Moore, Jacob Riis Biography website.

11. Museum of City of New York exhibit on Jacob Riis, 2016.

12. Anne M. Filiaci, www.Lillianwald.com

13. Ibid.

14. Museum of City of New York exhibit on Jacob Riis, 2016.

Chapter 8

1. *The House on Henry Street*, 203.

2. Ibid., 205.

3. Ibid., 143.

4. Ibid., 207.

5. Ibid., 220.

6. Ibid., 209.

7. Lillian Wald, *Windows on Henry Street*, 216.

8. Jean Hardin Fairleigh, "I Speak for Four Million," journal unknown.

Chapter 9

1. President Woodrow Wilson's Speech to Congress, April 2, 1917.

2. www.eyewitnesstohistory.com/wilsonwar.htm.

3. Washington Post. "Women Foes of War" *Washington Post.* January 11, 1915, 1-3.

4. "Profiles: Rampant but Respectable," *The New Yorker*, December 14, 1929.

5. "Seeing Red," Wald papers, Box 88, Columbia University Medical Library, Rare Book and Manuscript Library.

6. Lillian Wald, *Windows on Henry Street*, 307.

7. Letter to Miss Crandall, November 6, 1914.

8. American Union Against Militarism minutes and materials, Wald papers, Box 88, Columbia University Medical Library, Rare Book and Manuscript Library.

Chapter 10

1. Lillian Wald, *Windows on Henry Street*, 80.

2. Telegram to Senator Seeley, 1913, New York Public Library archives.

3. Ibid., 328.

4. Ibid., 232.

5. Ibid., 113.

6. Ibid., 114.

7. Ibid.

8. Wald to Lehman, February 16, 1939, Herbert Lehman papers, Columbia University.

9. Siegel, 167.

10. Franklin D. Roosevelt memorial service, 1940.

11. Dr. C.E. Winslow, "The Influence of Lillian Wald Reaches Round the Earth," Yale School of Medicine, School of Public Health.

References

Books:
Daniels, Doris Groshen. *Always a Sister: The Feminism of Lillian D. Wald*, Feminist Press at the City University of New York, New York, NY, 1989.
Duffus, R. L. *Lillian Wald, Neighbor and Crusader*, The Macmillan Company, New York, NY, 1938.
Siegel, Beatrice. *Lillian Wald of Henry Street*, Macmillan Publishing Company, New York, NY, 1983.
Wald, Lillian, *The House on Henry Street*, Henry Holt & Co., New York, NY, 1915.
Wald Lillian. *Windows on Henry Street*, Little, Brown & Co. Boston, 1933.
Williams, Beryl. *Lillian Wald: Angel of Henry Street*, Julian Messner, Inc., New York, NY, 1948.

Interviews and Tours:
Henry Street Settlement House website and interviews with staff and house tour
Visiting Nurse Service of New York website and interviews with staff

Papers:
The Federal Children's Bureau: A Symposium, Lillian Wald, New York, January 1909.
"The Influence of Lillian Wald Reaches Round the Earth," C.E. A Winslow, Yale School of Public Health.
Telegram to Senator Seeley, February 1914.
Wald letters to Jacob Schiff and various city officials, Wald papers, Reel 1, Box 1-2, New York Public Library Archives

Magazines:
"Profiles: Rampant but Respectable," *The New Yorker*, December 14, 1929.

Documentary:
100 Years of World War I documentary, Lionsgate Films, 2014.

Websites:
Eastman Kodak website, kodak.com
Henry Street Settlement website, henrystreet.org
Lillian Wald website, lillianwald.com
Metropolitan Life Insurance website, metlife.com/about

Museum Exhibits:
Exhibit on Jacob Riis in the Museum of the City of New York, 2016.

Suggested Further Reading

On Lillian Wald:
Daniels, Doris Groshen. *Always a Sister: The Feminism of Lillian D. Wald*, Feminist Press at the City University of New York, New York, NY, 1989.
Duffus, R.L., *Lillian Wald, Neighbor and Crusader*, The Macmillan Company, New York, NY 1938.
Siegel, Beatrice. *Lillian Wald of Henry Street*, Macmillan Publishing Company, New York, NY 1983.

Fictionalized Account of Lillian Wald:
Williams, Beryl. *Lillian Wald: Angel of Henry Street*, Julian Messner, Inc., New York, NY, 1948.

Autobiographies:
Wald, Lillian. *The House on Henry Street*, Henry Holt & Co., New York, NY, 1915.
Wald Lillian. *Windows on Henry Street*, Little, Brown & Co. Boston, 1933.

From Jacob Riis:
Riis, Jacob. *How the Other Half Lives*, Scribner's Books, New York, NY, First edition in 1890.
Riis, Jacob. *Children of the Poor*, Echo Library, New York, NY, First edition in 1892.
Riis, Jacob. *Battle with the Slum*, Dover Publications, New York, NY, First edition in 1902.
Riis, Jacob. *Children of the Tenements*, Forgotten Books, Location unknown, 1903.
Riis, Jacob. *Theodore Roosevelt*, "The Citizen," The Outlook Company, Location unknown, 1904.

On Jane Addams of Hull House:
Addams, Jane. *20 Years at Hull House*, 1935 first edition, most recent republishing is 2014.

Index